The Best of Retirement Planning

Compiled and Edited by Marion E. Haynes, Past President

International Society for Retirement Planning

This collection of articles from the journal of the International Society for Retirement

Planning provides a wealth of information for anyone wanting to know more about

retirement education, life planning and/or retiree relations.

Table of Contents

Preface

*T*he International Society for Retirement Planning (ISRP) was chartered in January 1975 and has served as the professional society in the field since then. In January 1994, it affiliated with the American Society on Aging.

The mission of ISRP is to enhance the awareness, knowledge, and skills of those involved in retirement planning, education, and counseling, life planning, and retiree relations. The objective of this effort is to enable members to provide the most effective retirement preparation services to mature adults.

Over the years as organizations responded to the need to provide planning for retiring employees, staff members were trained to conduct programs. Educational institutions and senior citizen organizations designed programs in response to the need. Private practitioners organized firms to provide seminars, programs, and materials for retirement planning.

ISRP's membership represents all of these fields. While many members are generalists with special skills in adult education, others specialize in one or more of the major aspects of retirement planning. These include: financial planning, estate planning, insurance, taxes, health and wellness, emotional adjustment, living arrangements, and travel and leisure.

The articles and reviews in this collection were originally published in Retirement Planning, ISRP's quarterly journal, from 1988 through 1993. The contribution these and other authors have made to the success of the Society and its journal is greatly appreciated. And, both members and non-members are encouraged to keep writing case history, research, and opinion articles. Through the sharing of experiences and ideas, ISRP will continue to grow in pursuit of its mission.

Marion E. Haynes, Editor

International Society for Retirement Planning

Retirement Planning is published quarterly by the International Society for Retirement Planning, an affiliate of the American Society on Aging. Cost of the publication is included in the annual membership fee. For information on membership, contact the Society's Administrative Office. Subscriptions are available to non-members at an introductory price of $19.95 for four (4) issues. Contact the Editorial Office for subscription information.

The Editorial Board welcomes unsolicited articles on a broad range of topics informative to practitioners in the fields of retirement and life planning, education and counseling, and retiree relations. Articles accepted for publication are subject to editing for clarity and to meet space limitations. Send articles to the Editorial Office.

Administrative Office
833 Market Street, Suite 511
San Francisco, CA 94103
(415) 974-9631

Editorial Office
1616 Long Ridge Road
Stamford, CT 06903
(203) 329-1818

1

INTRODUCTION

An Overview of Retirement Planning

by Marion E. Haynes

One million Americans retire each year and this number will double in the next ten years as the Baby Boom Generation begins to retire. Many of these people are unprepared for what lies ahead.

Old images of retirement no longer are valid. Retirement today is different from what it was for prior generations. No longer is it a relatively short time at the end of life to take it easy. Today, retirement is a substantial period of active living for those who have prepared. This new model is the result of two major factors.

The first is the number of Americans who are living longer. At the turn of the century, the average life expectancy for men was 48 years. Today that number has grown to 74. As a result of better medical care, improved diet, and increased interest in physical fitness, more people are reaching the ages of 65, 70, and older in excellent health. The activities and attitudes of a 70 year old today are about the same as a 50 year old a decade or two ago.

The other factor is a well defined trend toward earlier retirement. For example, in 1948, 50% of American men age 65 and older were actively engaged in the workforce. In 1989, this number had dropped to only 16%. Today, retirement at age 65 is more myth than reality.

As a result of these changes, today's retirees are younger and healthier than their predecessors. Their children are reared, their careers are complete, and they are ready to enjoy the fruits of their labors. But, to be financially, physically, and emotionally prepared to fully enjoy these additional years requires careful planning and commitment to carry out those plans. That's where retirement planning comes in.

The Employer's Role in Retirement Planning

Clearly, retirement planning is a personal matter that must be carried out by the individual with the assistance of trained professionals. However, employers have a role in the process to educate employees on the need to plan and the array of topics needing attention and then motivate them to take action.

Two surveys illustrate the degree of involvement by employers in retirement planning. Buck Consultants completed a survey of 386 companies in 1989. They found that 38% of the respondents had on-going programs and 18% of those who did not have programs planned to start them within two years. The International Foundation of Benefit Plans completed a survey of 301 employers in 1990. They found that 31% had programs at the time of the survey and more than half of those who didn't, planned to.

Employers cite many reasons for getting involved in retirement planning. For example:

- The complexity of tax laws affecting retirement distributions makes it necessary to provide some assistance.

- It takes less time to sign up a pension applicant who has been involved in planning his or her retirement.

- Our retired employees continue to be consumers, stockholders, political advocates, and public relations messengers. We want them to retire with a strong positive attitude toward the company.

- We believe we can make a positive impact on retiree health care costs by offering programs on healthy lifestyles.

- After a career of 30 to 40 years, facilitating the transition to retirement seems like a fitting conclusion.

- We must stay competitive within our industry and retirement planning is getting to be commonplace.

The Scope of Retirement Planning

Retirement planning assistance can vary from providing reading material, providing audio or videotape/workbook packages, or providing computer software, to conducting seminars and workshops. The subjects covered vary from a detailed review of company retirement benefits, to financial planning including post-retirement budgeting, estate planning, health and well being, and emotional adjustment.

This diversity has lead to the designation of three levels of programming:

- **Basic:** Assistance at this level is limited to employer retirement benefits and Social Security.

- **Intermediate:** *Assistance at this level adds financial planning with a focus on post-retirement budgeting, taxation of retirement benefits, estate planning, and how to select and work with a financial advisor.*

- **Comprehensive:** *In addition to the topics covered at the basic and intermediate levels, comprehensive assistance adds health and wellness, housing considerations, use of leisure time, and personal and family adjustments.*

ISRP recommends the comprehensive level of assistance.

Designing a Retirement Planning Program

If you are contemplating offering your employees assistance with retirement planning, you might start by engaging the services of a retirement planning professional. Such an individual can help you assess your needs, choose a cost effective approach, design a program that fits your circumstances, develop a communication plan to introduce the program, conduct sessions, and direct you to external resources.

Here are some of the key issues to think through:

- **Program Format:** *Will the program be based on written material, audio/video material, or lecture/discussions? Will it be self-study, private sessions, or group sessions?*

- **Participants:** *Which employees may participate—everyone, pension eligible, or minimum age, such as 45 or 50? Decide which non-employees may participate such as spouses, children, and/or advisors.*

- **Staffing:** *Decide whether to use staff or consultants to operate the program. Key roles to fill are designer, administrator, and presenter for group sessions.*

- **Scheduling:** *If you decide to have private or group sessions, you must decide when they will be conducted. First, decide if the program will be presented during one block of time or if it will be broken into two or more sessions. Then, decide if the sessions will be during working hours or not, and the time of day and days of the week that best fit your participants' needs.*

- **Location:** *Finally, pick the best available location. On-site meeting rooms are less expensive but encourage interruptions and tardiness. To promote the best learning environment, you may choose to use off-site facilities.*

A word of caution is worth noting at this point. You must design an unbiased program. This requires you to focus on information rather than advice and to be cautious of presenters who also market products. Many marketers will offer to make presentations without charge. The only reason they can afford to do this is to pick up business from your group of employees. This is probably not in your best interest in the long run. You expose yourself to potential liability by implicitly sponsoring the presenter's product or service.

Conclusion

Retirement planning is becoming increasingly important as Americans live longer in retirement. While such planning is the basic responsibility of the individual, employers are playing a more prominent role in the process. This employer involvement is driven by competition, return on investment, and ethical and/or moral considerations.

To get the best return for your effort, seek professional help in designing and presenting a comprehensive program. It will promote continuing loyalty of retirees, save time in retirement sign-up sessions, and you will be making a significant contribution to older Americans.

2

RETIREMENT PLANNING PROGRAMS

How to Develop a Retirement Program: Basic Tools, Techniques and Objectives

by Elizabeth S. Weiss

First, let me tell you a little about our company. We are a large manufacturer of electrical connectors. When we began pre-retirement planning 12 years ago, we had over 500 employees who were over age 50.

We continue to have a large population of older employees, many of them with many years of service. Our management is quite conservative when it comes to adopting new employee benefits.

The need for retirement planning became evident to me as I administered the pension plans. When I inquired of employees, "What are your plans for retirement?" the answers usually fell into four categories: going fishing, working around the house, visiting grandchildren, or traveling. Not much thought was given to what one was going to do beyond a superficial level.

There are many ways to disseminate information to employees, but each method is imperfect. You can distribute literature, but it usually is not read or understood.

Lectures are inspiring, but one week later, only 5% of what was said is recalled. One-on-one counseling is very time consuming and cannot cover all the issues.

Let me say, however, that now, with our retirement planning program to address the basics, our counseling is more effective and specific. We don't have to start from the ground up. We can concentrate on the person's particular need and requirements.

Our approach has been to cause employees to take responsibility for doing their own planning. We use a multifaceted workshop/ seminar series consisting of a facilitator, a resource authority or expert on each topic and, realizing that retirement is a family matter, we invite a small group of employees and spouses.

To convince management to put retirement planning into the annual benefits budget, the following goals were set forth:

Retirement planning would assist employees develop a favorable attitude toward retirement and help alleviate trauma over getting laid off.

It would demonstrate the company's concern for its employees and retirees.

We could put employees in touch with sources of further information and assistance.

Perhaps, more importantly, it would maximize the return in good will and understanding from the large expenditures which are made to our benefit programs such as retirement plans, savings plans and group insurance.

It would tend to minimize anxieties of employees over the future so that job performance is enhanced and fellow employees will not be adversely affected.

We use a format of weekly two-hour sessions for eight weeks. Eleven modules, or topics, are covered. If there is no other way, we consider weekend seminars for field personnel or distant facilities. Weekend workshops are exhausting for the facilitator; and for the participant, it is so much information at once, they can't absorb it all.

To start a new program, an effective advertising campaign is most important. We found that employees had several fears. Some were afraid that the company was just trying to get rid of them. "Does this mean that I am going to get laid off?" they asked. Some did not want to admit that they were approaching retirement. "I don't want anyone to know how old I am" was heard often.

It's as if they attended the sessions, someone would suddenly discover that they were there and think, "Well, let's just lay them off; they're going to retire, anyhow."

To counteract negative attitudes, we advertised in our company paper a complete description of the program, its goals and how it would operate well before the first session.

In addition, a personal contact was made to people in the shop who would be invited. We explained that everyone over 50 would eventually be invited, but that we had to start with the eldest employees first.

After the first group finished, we ran another article with photos of the participants to perpetuate the interest in pre-retirement planning and provide more facts.

We had prepared well and made sure all loose ends were tied down so nothing would rise up to become a detriment to the program. All the precautions and meticulous attention to detail paid off. Employees were delighted, word spread and now there is always a waiting list.

All the topics are important to our program, but the first session sets the tone for the rest of the series. It is essential to start off with a burst of positive excitement that will carry the momentum all the way to the end.

I would like to demonstrate how the first session might begin. It is an overview and introduction to the rest of the sessions. I begin by welcoming the participants with a special welcome to any spouses or other family members present and stress that their participation is just as significant as anybody

else is and to feel free to contribute whenever appropriate.

The purposes and objectives of the series are reiterated and defined. This program will spark the start of your own preparation for the future, it is stressed, whether it be retirement, or, just as importantly, not to retire.

This is an opportunity to locate, develop and view your own options for your own development. You can learn from your fellow participants through group discussion and sharing.

With approximately 25 people here, we have over 1,240 years of experience among us. With the group discussion method we are going to use, we can tap some of that experience.

We will become aware of professional, educational, recreational and other resources that are available.

We will learn to foster a positive attitude toward the future, develop support systems in the areas of friendships, pensions, social security, hobbies and interests, legal, financial and others.

You will not be given answers or advice, because only you know your own situation, but hopefully, you will learn to ask the right questions and where information can be obtained.

During these classes, plan to enlarge your present boundaries, consider new horizons, and to facilitate this, you are asked to try to sit in a different place each week or by a different person.

This is to allow you to be comfortable with different people and in various places, rather than staking out a private space and then not being comfortable outside that little area.

At about this point, we go around the circle, introducing ourselves in the following format: The leader goes first.

"Name? Where born? Family? Anything you wish to disclose about your education? Employer, if any? Hobbies and sports? My interest in pre-retirement planning is . . ."

This exercise lets the leader know each person's particular focus and bonds the group together.

Next, the format is explained. A book, *Think of Your Future,* is introduced. We have the participants read, in advance of each session, the material pertaining to the topic to be discussed. Some people learn best by reading, some by writing, some by listening and talking. In this group, we do all three.

We use audio visuals, and some short lectures, but the major part of the program uses case histories to stimulate group discussion.

Then there are Action Steps to say: Where are you now? Where do you want to go? and How do you get there? These are thinking and writing exercises where a person lists the highest priority items and sets a date to begin working on the plan. Then there is a schedule to check progress on each planning issue.

The group is asked to lay aside, at least temporarily, previously learned notions so a new, broadening outlook can be obtained. So we use the word "OLD" without reservations. If an old piece of art, an old coin, or an old piece of furniture can be valuable, why not an old person? Why indeed?

Next, the responsibilities of the discussion leader are set forth:

To plan as well as I can for a smooth running, beneficial program for everyone.

To prepare the best and most up-to-date materials for distribution.

To secure experts on each subject that are willing to share their experience and wisdom.

To give the group my best in energy and intention.

To facilitate the activities of learning; I am not a teacher in most of the sessions (exception, company benefits, my own area of expertise).

To present as many viable alternatives as possible for consideration.

To alert you to community resources you may not be familiar with.

By the same token, participant's responsibilities are given as:

Firstly, to be here. You cannot learn anything, you cannot share with others if you are not here.

Be on time.

Share your experience and opinions and feel free to disagree; differences are desirable; it is quite alright to attack someone's opinion, but do not attack the person.

Be candid, but do not air details of your personal problems.

Do the homework that is assigned; what you put into this is what you'll get out.

Learn to verbalize ideas about planning; discuss with others at home, at work and in social situations planning issues.

Learn to ask for help and who to ask it of.

After accumulating knowledge, **do your own thinking.**

Don't be a clone (especially to spouses: your ideas are separate, many times, from the one you're married to).

After this, the planning begins in earnest. The final session has everyone completing and turning in an evaluation form. Then it is time for graduation. There is a short commencement challenge to continue learning about all the subjects and sharing with others. Then we pass out certificates for the participants (and hugs for the leader) and a flower to each. The atmosphere is of a celebration.

Our program is constantly improving and evolving: Social activities for employees and retirees are planned. We have orchestrated a trip to the "Time of Your Life

Expo" on our own bus, which was wildly successful.

We have had follow-up lectures and additional mini-workshops to target various employee groups. We hope to offer more in the area of general life-planning as time goes along.

We have also begun making personnel more accessible to workers by spending time in the shop, at the actual workplace and in the areas where employees can talk to us on an informal basis about anything they wish.

Ms. Weiss is employed at ITT Cannon, Santa Ana, California.

Written Goals for a Retirement Planning Program Benefit Everyone: The Sponsoring Organization, the Program Planner and the Pre-Retirees

by Gloria Beebout

As people involved in retirement planning, we have an opportunity to help individuals as they make plans for up to one-third of their lives. When you think about it that way, as my 17-year-old daughter often says, "That's awesome."

Simply stated in the International Society for Retirement Planning materials, retirement planning is intended to assist employees and their spouses in preparing for retirement years. Programs are designed to provide awareness, techniques and viable options for enhancing the quality of life during retirement.

For the program planner, goals are important, first in setting written targets and later to serve as a means to evaluate the programs that have been developed. The following is a collection of goals broken into two categories, employer goals and individual participant goals.

Employer goals relate to bottom line issues such as productivity, staying competitive and restructuring as well as cultural issues that relate to the company as an organization of people.

The first goal is to spur employees to act. Retirement planning can empower people to make informed decisions and take action to make their plans work. Individuals are encouraged to take charge of the plan.

Second, programs should increase employee understanding and appreciation of company benefits. More choices and flexibility are being added to benefits through HMO's, PPO's, 401(k) plans, flexible life insurance and long-term care insurance.

Individuals must incorporate benefits into their plans along with Social Security, Medicare, personal savings and other financial products. A retirement planning program can encourage wise use of benefits before and after retirement. It can encourage participation in voluntary savings programs such as 401(k). A good program provides opportunities to ask questions which can lead to better understanding.

The next goal is to develop more self reliance in employees and retirees. Retirement planning can increase awareness of community resources and encourage employees to be responsible for their own retirement, including the employer benefits as one part of the plan.

Increasing employee productivity is another important goal. We often think we must increase employee productivity in order for programs to be approved. But how can retirement planning meet this goal?

Control of one's own plan can reduce the anxiety that may be associated with retirement. Tools that assist people with goal setting and implementation are identified. Eldercare issues that may affect up to 20 percent of employees can be discussed. Identification of potential resources may help working caregivers manage responsibilities.

Also, staying competitive with other employers can be accomplished with a successful plan. Retirement planning can provide a positive benefit at a low cost per employee. It can help the employer compete for and retain good employees. Positive relationships with future retirees can enhance the company image. After all, employees and retirees can be the best public relations people a company can have.

Helping older adults develop healthy lifestyles is another goal of a successful program. Physical, emotional and spiritual health are important at every age. Programs can reinforce positive aging which can impact use of benefits and productivity.

If your company is restructuring or down sizing, a good retirement planning program can help ease problems. What better place is there to assist employees to make informed decisions under current or future early retirement windows? This assistance may result in a better company image in the community at a difficult time.

It is a corporate responsibility to respond to an aging society, which a retirement planning program can help a company accomplish. Our demographics tell us that we are an aging population. Issues of aging discussed in retirement planning programs make us aware of opportunities to make a difference as a corporate member of our community.

Individual participant goals also must be part of program planning, development and evaluation. What do we want individuals to accomplish by participating in the retirement planning program?

- **Increase awareness of retirement planning subjects.** To be in control of their own circumstances, people need to know what questions to ask about financial planning, housing, legal issues, adjustments, health, retiree benefits, government programs and use of time. Changes in one area can affect another. For example, housing may be a financial issue. Health could affect use of time, legal issues and financial plans.

- **Develop goals appropriate to individuals' situations.** No two plans will be the same. They will be as different as the people doing the planning. Retirement plans can change and evolve as individuals approach and experience retirement.

- **Develop realistic expectations.** People should picture their own retirements. What they are doing, what they look like and how they feel may help them work toward more realistic expectations. How will they introduce themselves to others? People with differing pictures may begin to talk about their plans and why they are different.

- **Be aware of common concerns.** Recognizing that others have the same concerns may help people deal with their concerns more constructively.

- **Increase knowledge of benefits.** What happens to health insurance, pension, life insurance and other benefits at retirement? Does it make a difference if employees retire at younger ages? Can company service have an impact? Benefits information is essential to an individual planning for retirement.

- **Select appropriate retirement dates.** People are better able to weigh the pros and cons of different dates when they know what questions to ask and have developed a plan.

In conclusion, I want to borrow several phrases from well-known organizations and apply them to retirement planning—"Be prepared" (the Boy Scouts of America); "Think of your future" (AARP); and, "Make the best better" (4-H).

There are many goals appropriate for retirement planning. You may have others that fit your program or situation. Remember that effective goals are written down, used to develop programs and most important, used to evaluate and change those programs. Let's all take this opportunity and challenge to build excellence through goals in our retirement planning programs.

Ms. Beebout is a Senior Retirement Planning Counselor in the Benefit Plans Administrative Services Department at The Principal Financial Group, Des Moines, Iowa.

How to Teach Pre-Retirement Classes

by Robert O. Redd

My first exposure to retirement planning occurred six months before my Retirement Day. It included eight lectures presented by various authorities on retirement-related topics such as:

- The Myths of Retirement

- Financial Planning

- Social Security

- Health and Nutrition

- Use of Leisure Time

This is the usual menu of topics for the pre-retiree.

The program was sponsored by a local college and the presentations were held in a theater-like classroom. Needless to say, the participants' discussion opportunities were very limited. The audience was flooded with information and most of us left promptly after the lectures. Our heads were swimming with facts and anxiety levels were high.

Since I had been a management person for many years, I expected a more organized approach. I wanted more opportunity to integrate the information and more input from other pre-retirees, and even some insights from people who had retired.

I then began a crash course of self-education. I read every book and magazine article I could find about this major life change. It was difficult to come to an understanding of the real issues to be managed. It would have been very helpful to have had discussions with successful retirees, but they all appeared to be so busy it was hard to engage them. Most told me "it will work out in time." My pursuance was so extensive, I became "expert."

Finally "D" Day came—the office party, the signs and balloons—all the rites of passage.

After retirement, I decided to try to help others in their pre-retirement planning. I formed my own company and have been presenting programs for pre-retirees for several major corporations including AT&T and Amway Corporation.

In order to maximize the effectiveness of the programs, my wife and I have developed an environmental approach to the retiree's experience. Essential factual input is provided, but the programs go much beyond that to extended discussions by participants so that the many facets of the subjects can be explored. We strongly believe spouses should participate in the programs.

Careful consideration is given to the learning environment—type of seating, presenters'

teaching methods, arrangement of the participants in the room, and handout materials. There is no question that the attendees must be ready and at the "teachable moment" in their life. But the way the program is presented is critical to the effectiveness of the presentation.

Location

It is essential that the program location be easily accessible and comfortable for the group. We have been fortunate to have the use of a parlor in a large mansion that has been converted into an adult education center.

These warm, comfortable surroundings include the old marble mantel, ornate woodwork, and soft soothing draperies. Retirees and spouses receive name tags as they enter the reception hall and are then seated in comfortable chairs arranged in a circle. There are no tables or desks. The seating and arrangement of the participants has a major influence on the willingness of attendees to become involved in discussions.

We used "experts" to present specific subjects but, as moderator, I remained very much involved. The presenter sits in the circle and is open for questions at any time. If the presenter began to lecture, I interrupted him with a question.

Wherever possible, we have been using role-playing techniques to demonstrate a situation rather than discuss retirement challenges in the abstract. For example: A group of four people are gathered around a table discussing retirement.

One role player introduces the frustration she has with her husband being underfoot since he retired. She has lost her freedom. He has invaded her turf, etc.

The moderator then asks the students to react to the "problem." What can she do?

They develop ideas. Then the moderator suggests solutions.

Each role player presents a different challenge, e.g., health, financial, residence, travel. This role-play creates an involvement of the group with the moderator. They can experience the emotion the role player felt, and hopefully, relate the problem and alternative solutions to their lives. This approach is extended to many areas that require discussion.

Seating Arrangement

The circular arrangement of the class greatly facilitates discussion. There are many unspoken communications—a knowing smile, a frown, a gasp. Adult students are not "working for a degree." They are jealous of their time and will not continue to attend classes if they do not see the usefulness of the learning experience and they do not enjoy the meetings. The meetings become a social outing for the couples attending.

Participation helps them feel they have contributed to others and stimulates their interest in the subjects. It also increases the probability that they will explore the subjects in more detail for themselves.

Pre-retirement planning is an involved subject. It represents different challenges to each retiree and to the spouses. Some people need to focus on use of time, others on finances or health.

The classes need to be responsive to the needs of the members. Each group will have different intensity of concerns about the subjects. The instructor must be sensitive to the group dynamics and request feedback from the group.

The programs must be student oriented rather than content directed. And we have learned that the environment is a very important element in the learning experience.

Mr. Redd is a retired partner in the accounting firm of Seidman & Seidman, in Grand Rapids, Michigan.

Telling Pre-Retirees What It Will Be Like with Realistic Retirement Previews

by Sherry E. Sullivan, Ph.D.

By the year 2000, four of every ten Americans will be age 65 or older. As the population ages, organizations will be under increased pressure to provide employees with retirement preparation programs.

However, the basic format of retirement programs has changed relatively little in the last ten years and the quality of many of these programs is questionable. Most programs still do not provide information on the psychological aspects of retirement, such as attitudes toward retirement and family relations. Less than thirty percent of the retirement programs currently in use provide workers with more than insurance, health or financial planning information.

This is more distressing when one considers that the transition to retirement is probably the most traumatic work change that people make in their lifetimes. Ken Dychtwald, author of *Age Wave,* writes: "Many near-retirees are very concerned with the question of what to do next. Since we attach so much social value and worth to work and are, as a culture, uncertain of how we truly feel about leisure, people nearing retirement struggle with the fear of diminished purpose and activity. The suicide rate for American men is four times higher in retirement than in any other stage of life."

Because of the possibly devastating effects retirement can have on a person's self-worth, it is essential that organizations provide pre-retirees with a more comprehensive and authentic idea of what retirement living is like. One method is to use a Realistic Retirement Preview (RRP). RRP is based upon the organizational socialization technique called Realistic Job Preview and suggests that pre-retirees be informed of both the positive and negative aspects of retirement life.

How Traditional Retirement Programs Are Failing

A review of the research on retirement preparation programs indicates that a major objective of most of these programs is to increase people's positive attitudes toward retirement. Although having people look forward to retirement as a period of leisure and reduced stress may seem like an admirable goal, in reality it may instead be a mistake that results in retiree dissatisfaction and a sense of betrayal. For instance, many retirees complain that they are not adequately prepared for the stress and boredom that sometimes accompanies retirement.

People often experience a sense of loss and ambiguity when they retire from an organization. They are no longer "John Wilson—the top salesman with IBM" or "Sally Kellman—the manager of 25 retail clerks." Now they are just John and Sally, people who once worked, who once had others come to them for answers and who once made decisions that influenced people's lives.

Some retirees feel bitter toward their former employers for not providing them with a realistic idea about retirement.

One retiree I recently spoke with summarized these feelings of resentment when he remarked: "The company painted such a rosy picture of retirement. They did it so that us old guys would leave and make room for these young kids. . . . They don't tell you what it's really like. That you won't belong anymore. That your friends won't have time to talk anymore because they have a job to do. I'm doing okay now, but that first year was hard. The company talked about how I'd have time to travel and enjoy life. But they 'forgot' to tell me about the bad things . . . that I wouldn't be traveling all the time . . . and that I'd be in my wife's way around the house. Retirement is okay . . . but it's not quite what I thought it would be."

Feelings of resentment by former employees may be even stronger if an early retirement incentive buy-out program was offered in conjunction with a "Pollyanna" retirement preparation program. Workers may feel that the organization overemphasized the positive aspects of retirement in order to persuade them to accept the buy-out offer.

Therefore, providing employees with quality retirement preparation programs, such as RRP's, is not only ethically correct, but is a good business practice.

Retirement preparation programs send a message to current and future employees that the company is concerned about the well-being of its workers. Additionally, because of the changing demographics of our work force (e.g., increase in number of working mothers, shortage of younger workers), many organizations are asking retirees to return to work either full or part-time.

Companies would be wise not to alienate a large potential source of labor. By providing employees with quality retirement programs, companies can increase the loyalty and trust of pre-retirees who may later be asked to return to work.

What Is a Realistic Retirement Preview?

The Realistic Retirement Preview (RRP) is based on the newcomer socialization technique of Realistic Job Previews, (RJP). Dr. John Wanous from Ohio State University developed RJPs as a means of decreasing the high turnover rate of new employees.

RJPs work much like a medical vaccination. When we are vaccinated, a physician injects a small dose of germs into our bodies. Our bodies develop natural defenses so that we can defeat a large scale attack by these same germs. When RJPs are used, potential employees are given an idea of what working for the company would be like. Then they know about both the good and bad aspects of the job they are seeking. Providing job

candidates with a small "dose of reality," helps to deflate unrealistically high expectations and reduces the "reality shock" that is often experienced by organizational newcomers.

If these inflated expectations are left unchecked, dissatisfaction can occur after job candidates join the organization and their unrealistic expectations are not met. These dissatisfied and disillusioned employees often leave the firm after just a short tenure.

RJPs are supported by over thirty years of research and have been used in organizations ranging from banking institutions, telephone companies, insurance firms and the U.S. military.

The idea of the Realistic Job Preview can be extended to retirement socialization in the form of Realistic Retirement Previews, (RRP).

Like job candidates, retirees often develop fantasies of what they think retirement will be like. These fantasies may be quite accurate or they may be totally inaccurate. Research has found that pre-retirees who develop reasonably accurate ideas of what their retirement lifestyle would be like are better able to adjust to retirement than those who have unrealistic expectations.

Therefore, pre-retirees should be provided with realistic information about the retirement transition so they can adequately prepare and make the right choice as to when they will retire.

Presenting RRPs: How and By Whom?

RRP information can be presented in the form of brochures, videos, in-person counseling interviews, phased retirement or a combination of the four. While brochures are lower in cost than videos and can be re-read by the pre-retiree, there is no guarantee they will be read.

Video and counseling interview methods are not constrained by the reading levels of the pre-retirees. Counseling interviews permit flexibility in that the RRP can be tailored to the individual needs of the pre-retiree.

For example, if the pre-retiree plans to retire to a life of travel, the counselor may wish to devote additional time to helping the pre-retiree allocate financial resources for those plans and to discuss the special travel needs of older individuals.

In contrast, if the pre-retiree plans to return to work part-time, the counselor may wish to focus extra time on job search skills and the ways to overcome the problems people over 40 usually face when seeking employment.

The success of RRPs may be increased if they are presented by retired employees of the same company or occupation. Using retired people to act as peer counselors and trainers may enhance the acceptability of pre-retirement programs and increase participant trust and openness.

Finally, perhaps the best form of RRP is phased retirement. Phased retirement includes such programs as reduced working hours, extended leaves, sabbaticals, job sharing or reduced job responsibilities. Phased retirement permits employees to slowly disengage from their jobs. They can learn what retirement is first hand, testing different mixtures of work and leisure. Phased retirement permits people to develop non-work sources of satisfaction, such as hobbies and volunteer activities, while continuing to receive satisfaction from their jobs.

A recent Harris poll reported that 80% of workers aged 55 to 64 would prefer part-time employment over retirement. However, only approximately 10 to 20% of organizations provide any form of phased retirement.

Organizations may now wish to consider phased retirement programs because they solve a firm's labor supply problems. The Workforce 2000 report, as well as information from the Bureau of Labor Statistics, predict a shortage of younger workers for the decade. For example, in 1990, there will be 44% fewer in the age 18–25 age group than in 1980.

Conclusion

There has been some disagreement as to whether the purpose of pre-retirement programs should be to supply information or to aid in adjustment to retirement. Realistic Retirement Previews solve this dilemma by providing pre-retirees with accurate information that helps prepare them for the reality of retirement. Realistic Job Preview is an established tool for helping increase the job survival rates and satisfaction of new employees. Using a similar tool for retirement planning may increase the effectiveness of such programs, which benefits both employer and employee alike.

Dr. Sullivan is an assistant professor of management in the Fogelman College of Business and Economics at Memphis State University, Memphis, Tennessee.

Structuring a Retirement Planning Program in Your Company to Satisfy the Total Needs of the Retiree and Spouse

by Georgene M. Grattan

Before I begin to explain the different formats used at my firm to conduct retirement planning workshops for companies, I thought it would be appropriate to share my personal feelings regarding the subject of retirement planning.

People have characterized me as a very opinionated person. I have an opinion on most things. One such area I not only have a strong opinion about but I believe I really know is, this subject of retirement planning and how vitally important it is to have a comprehensive program for employees and that the program include the spouse.

I believe the program must get in touch with all of the real issues of retirement. Not just the financial issues but the total picture. The picture that will be framed and hung on the wall reflecting all of the feelings, the insecurities, the attitudes, the real scares and the goals that take place in, before and during retirement.

A verse from a popular song is: "Life is much more valuable, when there is less of it to waste"...

When I turned 50, a friend asked, "What was different when you turned 50 versus when you turned 40?" My response: "I have always been a realist and very much in touch with my feelings, fears, expectations and goals. However, when I turned 50, I became very real!"

As planners for the past 30 years, my husband and I have always had a financial plan for our present direction and for the future. With four sons in college at the same time, it was vital to have a plan and to plan well ahead of time for that event. But now at age 50, I started looking at the real of:

My health (physical, emotional and mental).

Wellness over the long term.

Exercise.

My relationship with my spouse and other social relationships.

Our financial security.

At age 50, I now knew that I could put a number on how long I would live. Perhaps another 30 years. Well, I've been married that long. Our oldest son is 29 years old. All of our lives we could measure how long we would probably live because the statistics have always been available. Men live until they are 79 and women live until the age of 81. We also know how long our grandparents lived and if our parents are still alive and in good health, we can assume, short of an accident, we should live at least that long.

We now very realistically can start measuring "Time to do's": all of the hiking, skiing, golfing, just relaxing, the hugging of the grandchildren, the loving and the living. Probably most importantly, we can and must now deal with: How long will the money last? We could have and should have measured it all along but we didn't deal with it here in our real consciousness.

I believe that it is where the reality of the mid-life re-evaluation was recognized (we don't call it crisis). We start to deal with what I have done so far, what haven't I done, what do I want to do, can I afford it in time and money?

How do we as corporate consultants look at the question of structuring a pre-retirement program to satisfy the real and total needs of the retiree?

Years ago, planning wasn't a formal program. It was several meetings scheduled with key executives of the corporation and discussions regarding, (almost exclusively) tax planning questions: "How much do I need to retire and how long will I be able to maintain my standard of living?" The pension benefits were not as complicated and diverse as they are today. However, the questions were still pretty much the same.

The specific pre-retirement planning programs conducted by my firm now take one or more of the following formats:

For Top Executives: We have maintained the format I have used with top executives since I started 30 years ago. We conduct one-on-one meetings with the executives and their spouses. It normally takes place at a resort for the weekend, or at some location where they can be away from their phones and other distractions. We meet several times over the weekend to discuss all of the issues surrounding the financial decisions of retirement. They are asked to bring all their financial records—tax returns, bank and brokerage statements, expense vouchers, etc.

We analyze the information from the clients, and through modeling with the numbers, produce a completed plan with recommendations.

In this consultation, we spend enough time with the couple to get to know one another and address their financial concerns without delay. While they are spending some time together and enjoying golf or other activities, we analyze where they are numerically and where they want to be.

In many instances, we bring a portable computer with us and an office technician. The client, at the end of this weekend retreat, will have very substantive directions.

We generally will have additional time to focus on other issues, with input from experts, such as life and aging attitudes.

Follow-up meetings are scheduled a week or two later at our corporate office.

For Mid-Management: We generally conduct small group sessions with no more than 15 couples at a time. We suggest the total program should take place two nights a week for three weeks and cover all of the salient issues surrounding retirement, not just the financial issues. It has also been offered in two or three full day workshops or over a week-end at a local hotel.

This audience is composed of employees in the mid 50s and early 60s. We hope in the near future to see people ages 35 to 55, to get them into the planning mind set at an earlier age.

Sessions are partly in lecture format and partly with hands-on participation of the attendees. They are asked to answer financial questions regarding their own personal circumstances. They fill out forms and we work with them to calculate their own personal numbers.

We walk them through the calculation of net worth, cash flow before and during the projected retirement years, discuss some of the alternative types of securities available, the tax consequences of the pension and IRA distributions, portfolio construction, asset allocation or diversification, how to calculate the needed funds during retirement to cover standard of living, estate planning and insurance exposure.

We calculate inflation, expectations of growth and income, and calculate how long these dollars will last (how many years can they live comfortably on their assets after they stop earning). If there is a surplus, we can always find a way to spend the extra funds. If there is a shortfall, we can then target what to do to make up that short-fall in increased earnings, altering where and/or how much dollars are spent or look at other alternative retirement options.

Large Group Workshops: Some compa-nies have asked us to conduct workshops for larger groups.

We call them workshops, not seminars, because we expect attendees to participate in the discussion and work through their own numbers. We have self-quizzes through-out the workshop so that the participants have real hands-on experience with their own numbers and what they mean to their financial security.

We have found that pre-retirees at almost any level do not always realize the expanded choices available to them at retirement.

There is no end to the information avail-able on the subject of retirement. I don't believe there is a better time in history to be reaching or planning for retirement.

We also have long-held retirement deci-sions which now need to be re-evaluated. Again, we stress that even though the finan-cial questions are extremely important, they are not the total picture.

One of the programs where we ask our attendees' participation, is called the LifeStyle Inventory. This report addresses all of what we consider the vital issues in retirement planning, in addition to finan-cial security. This can be completed by the participant sitting in front of the computer and responding to the questions. The report is printed immediately after the last question is completed. Or it can be admin-istered by the written questionnaire with the results presented to the participant at a later time.

We have another program called Riskscan that targets specifically the health risks the individual is personally exposed to, living in today's society, and the risk associated with his/her personal lifestyle.

The retirement planning sessions are nor-mally conducted in a variety of formats and time structures. In addition to the formats discussed, we have also covered the topic in an afternoon or lunch hour, depending on the request of the corporate sponsor.

Ms. Grattan is with the firm of Grattan, Boyd & Associates, a registered investment advisory firm in Glendale, California.

It's Never Too Early to Start Planning for Retirement

From Synergy, *Wisconsin Electric Power Co.*

At an evening session of the Wisconsin Electric pre-retirement preparation and planning course, 40 people huddle over a case study of the fictional Walkers, poring over financial statements and analyzing saving and spending habits. Their assign-ment: What should the Walkers do to prepare for retirement?

Sell the house, suggests one couple. Quit entertaining so much, offers another. More ideas tumble out: Dump the coin collection. Sell the second car.

"With just one car, you're going to have to decide if his fishing or her bridge club is more important," Joe Schuster, the coordinator of WE's Pension Benefits, responds to the car-selling suggestion. "Sounds like trouble to me." And the coin collection? "That's what Mr. Walker was going to do in retirement." One by one, he counters every suggestion.

Later Schuster explains. "The point is, the Walkers don't have to change anything," he says. "Sure, they could increase their income with different investments. They don't have to decrease living expenses any more than they want to. They don't have to change their lifestyle."

Schuster says many employees spend more time planning for a two-week vacation than their own retirement. Retirement can offer exciting possibilities as well as potential problems. Planning puts you in control of your future and helps shape retirement into a satisfying experience.

To help employees prepare for retirement, Schuster leads a pre-retirement preparation and planning course, which is offered to employees who have reached age 55. The class, which includes spouses, meets once a week for six consecutive weeks to help those approaching retirement age gain a better understanding of retirement issues:

The company retirement plan—when you can retire, how retirement benefits are calculated and what forms of payment are available;

Other company benefits—health insurance, dental insurance, life insurance, Tax Reduction Act Stock Ownership Plan and employee savings plans;

Social Security benefits—for yourself and your spouse; disability and survivor benefits;

Tax planning and preparation;

Legal issues—wills, trusts, power of attorney and durable power of attorney;

Financial planning—sources of income, investment options and Individual Retirement Account (IRA) rollovers;

Housing alternatives;

Funeral arrangements;

Wellness—medical care, nutrition and exercise.

Where WE Benefits Fit In

For WE employees, the company's retirement benefits, savings and stock plans can account for a large portion of retirement income. The retirement benefit, which is paid entirely by WE, is designed to provide income in addition to the monthly benefit they may receive from Social Security and their savings.

Eligible employees receive a monthly benefit check. The amount is based on factors such as the number of years in the plan, wage level, retirement age and form of payment. As you near retirement, the Pension Division shows you how your benefit is calculated and explains the various payout options available.

The company also offers voluntary savings plans that employees may want to consider for retirement investments. These are 401(k) plans that allow employees to invest wages in Wisconsin Energy Corp. common stock or various investment funds. Investment options range from conservative choices such as fixed rate-of-return income funds to more volatile and risky growth stock funds. Contributions are tax-deferred.

Like any investment, these plans involve a certain amount of risk, but the tax advantages make such plans a favorite recommendation of many financial planners.

What about Social Security?

They are told not to count on federal government Social Security to finance the bulk of their retirement years like it did for their parents or grandparents. Although benefits do increase to account for inflation, chances are they'll represent only a small portion of their necessary retirement income.

Changing demographics promise to further burden the system. Today, some 12% of Americans are over 65, and by 2030, when most baby boomers have reached retirement, that figure will swell to nearly 25%. The federal government is already searching for ways to stretch future Social Security dollars. Under present law, if you're under age 32, you'll have to wait until age 67 to collect full Social Security benefits.

WE's Pension Division helps employees calculate their Social Security benefit as they near retirement. They are encouraged to obtain a current statement of their Social Security earnings from the Social Security Administration.

Building a Nest Egg

Some of the ways to supplement retirement income include 401(k) plans, IRAs, life insurance annuities, mutual funds, money market accounts, stocks and bonds. They are told to be wary of salespeople promising "risk-free, high-yielding" investments. They are advised to get a second opinion before committing any money and not become one of the horror stories involving someone who lost a nest egg on a "sure thing."

Investing at a young age offers advantages. Unfortunately most employees in their 20s find it difficult to save. For some, the concept of saving just seems too premature— especially when there are stereos, new wardrobes and cars to buy.

Employees are encouraged to try to establish a savings plan. Before thinking about long-term savings, though, they are advised to stash some cash for emergencies.

Financial planners suggest six months' worth of salary in a readily accessible account such as a certificate of deposit or a standard savings account. Next, employees are told to earmark some money for their future. Start modestly if you have to, say the experts, but do start. Because you won't be retiring for several decades, years of compounding interest will turn even a small nest egg into a nicely feathered nest. Use a long-term tax-deferred vehicle like a 401(k) or an IRA, if eligible. 401(k) contributions reduce your taxable income and accrue earnings on a tax-free basis.

IRAs also provide a tax reduction if you do not exceed income level requirements, but even if you don't qualify, you can still accrue tax-free earnings.

In your 30s: Making More and More Ends Meet

Your 30s are typically a time of growing children and growing bills. With mortgage payments, food bills, clothing expenses and the specter of college tuition, it's no wonder that the average savings rate in the U.S. is a paltry 3.7% of income.

Computer programs can crank out specifics, but a good rule of thumb is to set aside about 10% of your income in a tax-deferred retirement account. That percentage escalates quickly the longer you wait to begin saving.

Piggy bank-style saving is no longer enough. Building wealth is futile if your investment strategy is overly conservative.

In your 30s, most experts agree, you can weather a bumpier investment ride and more risk since retirement is a long way off. After all, so-called conservative investments may prove even riskier down the road if they can't keep pace with inflation.

In Your 40s: Peak Earning Power, Peak Saving Years

As your earnings increase, so should their retirement investments. If possible, you should put away the maximum allowable by law in a 401(k) (15% of base wages or a maximum or $8,728 for 1992) or an IRA ($2,000 per year).

Those in their 40s, however, have the dubious distinction of belonging to the "sandwich generation"—many balancing the costs of maturing children (translation: college) and maturing parents (translation: elder care).

In Your 50s: Shifting Assets and Gears

As retirement grows larger on the horizon, you are encouraged to review your overall financial plan and look into any future insurance needs, such as long-term health/nursing care. Some experts suggest shifting some money into more cautious fixed-income investments at this age. Since you will be tapping into some of the money within the next 5 to 10 years, they may want to start smoothing out the bumpy ride associated with all-growth-stock portfolios.

In Your 60s: Handling the Home Stretch

Once you have decided on a retirement date, the WE Pension Division visits you at your home to review the various forms of payments provided by the retirement plan, continuation of health and life insurance, application for Social Security benefits, tax concerns and savings plans distributions.

"The purpose of this visit is not to tell employees what to do," says Schuster, "It's to provide information so they can more intelligently make their own financial decisions."

About 2½ months prior to retirement, another meeting is held to sign necessary papers, review calculations and sign applications for continued health coverage. This meeting also is used to show how to report retirement benefits for income tax purposes, sign requests for federal and state income tax withholding from benefit checks and sign requests for distribution of savings plans assets and show how they can be treated for tax purposes.

Even if retirees are confident they've amassed sufficient funds for retirement, they are asked to consider if they are as well-prepared emotionally. Even the most hobby-laden, athletic travel buff with a healthy marriage is bound to face a few emotional concerns upon giving up a long standing way of life.

"Retirement takes a lot of adjustment for some," notes Schuster. "But, invariably, I see those same people a few years into retirement, and they look so happy. The stress is gone, and they're doing what they want when they want."

As on the financial front, the key to emotional health in retirement is planning. He advises, "Don't wait until the eve of your retirement date to start thinking about what you'll do with your free time. Begin building on your present interests, or acquire new ones.

"Explore volunteer work. Sign up for a class. Plan to travel.

"Start that planning as early as possible and you—like the fictional Walkers—can enjoy a rosy, rewarding retirement."

Adapted from Synergy, *publication for employees of Wisconsin Electric Power Co., Milwaukee, as an example of this firm's efforts to get younger employees to consider their futures. Used by permission of the editor.*

Lifeplan, with Federal Funding, Aspires to Be a National Model for a Retirement Planning Program, to Be Shared with Other Communities

by M. Lynn Hire

As America approaches the twenty-first century, the need for employers to offer comprehensive preretirement planning becomes more critical.

According to a recent report issued by the staff of the "Kiplinger Washington Letter," the 65-plus age group will rise from about 29 million, or 12% of the population now, to 13% by the year 2000. The number of seniors is expected to nearly double by 2010, when the first of the Baby Boomers hit retirement in large numbers.

It has been projected that for every two individuals who are working in 2010, there will be three who are retired. Some experts say it may be unrealistic to expect the Social Security system to support this burgeoning population of seniors.

In response to the aging trend, officials at the Metropolitan Community Colleges (MCC) in Kansas City have developed a cost-effective program to assist employers in their efforts to prepare today's employees for tomorrow's retirement years.

The community education program, called Lifeplan, focuses on the social, psychological, financial and medical aspects of aging. By utilizing community volunteers from a variety of professional fields, Lifeplan provides preretirement training to individuals 35 and older, through public and employer-sponsored seminars.

Although most companies provide some type of retirement preparation information for employees, few programs exhibit concern for the "total person" during retirement years, observed Dr. Wayne Giles, vice-chancellor of educational services at MCC.

"Lifeplan provides ongoing preparation, beginning early in life, for the inevitable lifestyle changes that occur after retirement. Representatives from private sector businesses are becoming more interested in Lifeplan as an affordable component of their employee benefits packages," Dr. Giles said.

"The variety of topics and the number of volunteers allows Lifeplan to present a comprehensive, flexible program at a very nominal cost—less than $50 per person. The volunteers are selected from the ranks of the community professionals including physicians, attorneys, accountants, etc., for their expertise and their ability to communicate with the seminar attendees," explained Larry Spohn, Lifeplan director.

More than 400 federal employees attended a Lifeplan preretirement seminar last fall in Kansas City. Participants had the opportunity to learn from a variety of presenters, speaking on topics ranging from choosing health care services, to estate planning, to mid-life crisis and travel. The seminar attracted employees in their 30s, interested in developing sound financial planning strategies for their future, as well as those individuals only months away from retirement, hoping to discover new avenues for realizing personal and financial satisfaction.

"The first step toward planning ahead is to first realize that we will all grow older and retire. We never really picture ourselves as older.

"When it does occur to us, few of us really have the necessary skills to plan effectively," said David Monson, vice president of operations for HealthNet in Kansas City.

Mr. Monson is a former director for the Missouri Department of Aging and is one of 15 members on the local Lifeplan Advisory Board.

Lifeplan, now in its second year, is funded by a federal grant from the Administration on Aging. The program is being developed as a national model, to be made available to other community colleges across the nation, as interest in preretirement planning escalates.

By offering Lifeplan through the community college network, as opposed to commercial marketing, officials hope the program will remain affordable and accessible for widespread implementation.

According to Spohn, MCC of Kansas City plans to host a national conference to introduce Lifeplan to two-year colleges interested in adopting the program for use in their respective communities. The conference, a model of Lifespan curriculum, will feature presentations, workshops and classes presented by a consortium of experts from various groups.

The Lifeplan staff at MCC is currently developing a "complete package" consisting of a set of video products as well as printed material and instructional guides which will eventually be distributed to other two-year colleges. As the demand for the program increases, Lifeplan will be replicated and shared with other communities. Public

service announcements, brochures and a national newsletter will be disseminated to personnel and benefits managers in communities where Lifeplan is implemented, to generate interest in preretirement education. According to Spohn, Lifeplan was designed to incorporate flexibility with affordability and comprehensiveness. The purpose, he said, is to make life planning available to the community under any circumstance.

One aspect of this flexibility is the "central" program designed to meet the needs of small businesses, by presenting seminars on a scheduled basis in a central facility, allowing small business the opportunity of referring qualified employees to the program.

As the turn of the century approaches and the Baby Boom generation begins thinking about retirement, American society will be forced to come to terms with the impending age wave and its effects upon virtually every aspect of life.

"I cannot think of an area that aging won't touch upon—employment, finance, housing, healthcare, politics, marketing and several other aspects of modern society will be altered drastically," explained aging consultant David Monson, former executive director of the Missouri Division of Aging and former director of the Illinois Department on Aging.

This senior boom, as it is called, is picking up momentum and is expected to continue until 2010, when, for the first time, the number of retired persons will exceed the number of individuals in the workforce, by a three to two ratio. In light of these facts, the growing importance of retirement planning becomes apparent.

Successful planning will be the key to satisfying, secure and productive retirement years. This burgeoning wave of seniors simply won't be content to let life pass them by. A complete understanding of the societal changes that will inevitably occur during the next twenty to thirty years, along with long-range planning and preparation, will ensure the active, healthy, vigorous and dynamic lifestyle to which tomorrow's seniors will aspire, Monson said.

According to Monson, trends in employment are already rapidly changing, as older workers extend their service to the company beyond the established retirement age, or in some cases, retrain in a completely different area to embark upon a second career, after a first retirement.

"In addition, I think we will witness a tremendous effort to bring older Americans back into the workforce to fill openings at some of the flexible-schedule service-related jobs, that at one time were quickly scooped up by a surplus of high school kids with extra time on their hands," Monson said.

Gerontologist Key Dychtwald, Ph.D., who recently delivered the keynote address at a conference sponsored by the American Society on Aging, believes a cyclical approach to planning one's life is gradually replacing linear lifeplanning.

It used to be that an individual's life was divided into three distinct phases, each designated for a specific activity.

In linear lifeplanning, learning, working and death were certain.

Beginning now, however, and moving into the future, lifeplanning will occur in a cyclical pattern, which may be repeated several times during one lifetime. The cycle will consist of three interchangeable stages: learning, working and leisure, he says. Cyclical lifeplanning offers individuals the opportunity to retrain in midlife for a new career, or possibly take a year off, to alter or refine future plans. "Continuing education and adult learning programs at colleges and universities will become increasingly popular among the senior population," Monson predicts.

Contrary to popular belief, older Americans are very capable and enthusiastic learners, as well as teachers, Monson says. As a result, mentor programs are expected to become widely promoted in the corporate world as an effective method of training younger employees.

The changes expected to occur in the arenas of work and education are just two examples of the tremendous lifestyle shifts that an aging population is likely to create. According to Monson, it is in the field of healthcare that some of the most dramatic changes will be witnessed.

"Improvements in healthcare are allowing us to live longer and better lives. In the past, people didn't age, they died," explained Dychtwald.

Life expectancies are expected to increase drastically in the next century. In fact, researchers are now projecting that babies born in the year 2000 will live to an average age of 96 years. It will be the oldest of the old whose population increases most significantly. Experts say that by the year 2050, there will be more than 16 million Americans over age 85.

For those involved in preretirement planning, awareness of likely trends in healthcare is a must.

Rising costs, combined with a growing population of elders in need of longterm healthcare for chronic illnesses, are likely to result in financial catastrophe for hospitals and insurance companies, Monson said.

"In some countries, rising costs have created a trend of rationing healthcare among the elderly. To some, it's purely an issue of economics. We only have so much money, so we must use it as wisely as possible," Monson said.

"We have the capability to keep someone alive for years. Now, we have to come up with a moral decision on how to deliver medical care," he continued.

Home healthcare and elderly daycare are options that are too often overlooked.

Experts say that more than 25 percent of nursing home residents do not actually require the full range of services provided in the long-term care environment. One of the most promising businesses of tomorrow, that futuristic companies are making plans to capitalize on, is independent housing for the elderly.

These housing facilities will be designed specifically to meet the needs of the elderly resident. Generally one level structures, the units will often be located adjacent to medical facilities, providing nursing care to residents who need limited assistance.

Awareness of these housing and healthcare trends is especially valuable to middle-aged women beginning to plan for their retirement years. Demographers are predicting that women will continue to outlive the men.

According to Dychtwald, for every 100 women over the age of 85, only 42 men over 85 are still living.

A recent report issued by Pre-Retirement Education Planning for Mid-Life Women (PREP), conducted by Long Island Universities, states that roughly 50 percent of all employed women and 80 percent of retirement-age women have no pension eligibility. In addition, PREP has revealed that 70 percent of the elderly poor are women.

Obviously the graying of America impacts more heavily on women. As a result, early planning is a must, in order to afford necessary healthcare and satisfactory housing in the future.

The elderly population will continue to grow in power and wealth, Monson said, estimating that today's seniors control 90 percent of the nation's wealth and 95 percent of all political and corporate power. Older Americans, frequently referred to as the American gerontocracy, consistently turn out at the polls on election day. As companies seek to design and sell marketable products and services, and as politicians develop their campaign platforms and slogans, you can bet they'll be paying increasingly more attention to the senior population, Dychtwald predicts.

"As we sort through the facts, I think it's important to look at the positives related to aging. Obviously, seniors have the potential of being a major force in our population. Preparation and planning for tomorrow will allow the Baby Boomers of today to maintain a comfortable and productive lifestyle in the future, when they reach retirement," Monson said.

Lynn Hire is Lifeplan Communication's coordinator at Metropolitan Community Colleges in Kansas City, Missouri.

3

FINANCIAL TOPICS

Americans Feel Unprepared for Retirement, Attitude Survey Shows

by Steven A. Scott

Americans are deeply worried that they won't have enough money in retirement, according to a national survey commissioned by IDS Financial Services.

And baby-boomers, who are most worried, may have to either work longer, save more of their income now or live on less in retirement than they planned.

The independent survey, conducted by the Daniel Yankelovich Group, Inc., of New York, found that funding a secure retirement is Americans' top financial priority.

Despite how important they think saving for retirement is, however, only half of the 1,400 respondents say they are doing well at it. Three-quarters are concerned that they will have to lower their standard of living in retirement. Half think they will have to work at least part-time in retirement to make ends meet. Almost one-fifth fear that, in the worst case, they might be homeless in retirement.

Americans are clearly uneasy about being able to afford the kind of retirement they want.

Although 94 percent of those surveyed said being financially independent in retirement is important to them, only 38 percent said it is very likely they will achieve that independence.

Baby boomers are particularly pessimistic about how they'll live in retirement, about the future of Social Security, about inflation eroding their retirement savings and about achieving financial independence.

On average, people in the survey estimated they would need about $36,000 per year in today's dollars to live on in retirement. An IDS financial analysis shows that even those with some savings and some pension would have to save up to $500 a month to generate that income over an average life span.

Baby boomers want a higher retirement income than the older respondents in the survey—$42,000 compared to $32,000—and they also want to retire earlier—60 compared to 62. But, to accomplish that, they would have to save well over $500 a month during their working years. Those baby boomers who can't afford that may find themselves working longer before retiring.

Other major findings of the IDS Retirement Survey:

- Even though half of the people surveyed said they don't think Social Security will amount to much by the time they retire, people still are counting on Social Security to provide one-fourth of the money they'll need in retirement.

- The majority of Americans say they want and expect more information and help from their employers on saving for retirement.

- Almost three-quarters want the full tax deduction for IRAs restored.

- One-fourth of those surveyed are concerned about depending on a child or relative for support.

- Well over half of those surveyed said they haven't spent enough time on retirement planning, and just under half said they wished they'd started saving for retirement earlier.

The survey shows people are thinking about retirement, even if most feel they're not doing enough to prepare for it.

Retirement planning will become the number one financial concern of the 1990s as more baby boomers reach retirement planning age. Saving for retirement can seem daunting on top of other expenses, but it can be done with realistic goals, careful planning and saving.

The IDS Retirement Survey, an extensive mail questionnaire, was completed by 1,400 people who are employed, between the ages of 35 and 64 and who have household incomes of $30,000 or more.

Steven A. Scott, is a financial planner with IDS Financial Services, Inc. in Irvine, California.

Options When Receiving a Lump Sum Distribution

by Lawrence H. Wilson, Jr.

If you are about to retire or change jobs or your employer is terminating a retirement plan, you may be eligible to receive a "lump-sum distribution" as defined by the Internal Revenue Code. Such a distribution may be substantial and may represent one of the cornerstones of your retirement security. So consider your options carefully before making a decision regarding distributions.

Two main options need to be addressed. While there are many IRS rules and regulations concerning retirement plan distributions that you should discuss with your tax advisor, your questions will generally lead you to consider two options:

- Should I take my distribution and pay taxes now?

- Should I roll my distribution over into an IRA?

The Advantages of Paying Taxes Now

If you decide not to roll your distribution over into an IRA, you will pay taxes in the year you receive the distribution and have the remainder to invest as you please without regard to further IRS rules and regulations.

The main benefit of paying taxes on the distribution now is that you may be eligible for a special tax treatment of five- or ten-year forward averaging or capital gains treatment. If that is the case, you may pay a lower tax rate than usual on the distribution.

Otherwise, the distribution will be taxed at your ordinary income tax rate.

The Advantages of Rolling Over Distributions

Your second option is to roll your distribution over into an IRA. This alternative assures that your assets will continue working to provide for you during your retirement years.

The main benefit of rolling over a distribution is that you would continue to defer current taxes on these assets until they are withdrawn from the IRA account.

The advantages of tax-deferred growth are considerable. All assets in your IRA, including the earnings on your rollover, will continue to grow free from current taxes until you begin distributions from the account. Under current IRS regulations, you need not begin receiving distributions for your IRA until you reach age 70½.

Rollover Facts to Keep in Mind

As you can see, there are significant advantages to IRA rollovers. Now let's consider some additional important facts about rollovers.

- You have only 60 days from the receipt of your lump-sum to roll over distributions to an IRA.

- You may roll over all pre-tax contributions and all earnings from the distributions from your employer's plan. However, you may not roll over any after-tax contributions.

- Regardless of whether it is deductible, you may make your annual $2,000 IRA contribution. However, mixing regular IRA contributions with your rollover account will prohibit you

from rolling your distributions back into another employer's qualified plan in the future.

- With a contributory IRA, you can only put in cash, but with a rollover IRA, if you receive non-cash assets as part of your distribution, you can put them in directly. For example, if you receive shares of your employer's stock, you do not have to sell them in order to put them in your rollover IRA.

- You may take distributions from your IRA rollover account at any time. However, if you are under age 59½, you will be subject to a premature distribution penalty, unless the distribution is on account of death or disability, or takes the form of substantially equal periodic payments as defined by IRS code section 72(T).

The IRA rollover account provides you with an opportunity to continue building your assets while you defer income tax until you begin receiving distributions during retirement when you may be in a lower tax bracket than during your working years. This could mean the difference between living simply and living well during retirement.

Before deciding which tax-saving strategies best meet your objectives, it is a good idea to evaluate your complete personal financial situation. Be sure to consult your personal tax advisor before making any tax-related investment decisions.

Mr. Wilson, Jr. is Senior Vice President, Investments for Dean Witter Reynolds, Inc., Dallas, Texas.

Asset Allocation: Look Before You Leap

by George E. Ginther, LUTCF

Asset allocation has been a buzz word in personal finance for several years. At times it's been used by some as a marketing ploy to attract reluctant investors still frightened by Black Monday in 1987, and more recently, by Friday 13th, in 1989.

But is asset allocation really a novel investment strategy, or is it just a fancy name for "diversifying your investments?"

Whether you've already jumped on the bandwagon or are still waiting on the sidelines, here is the bottom line on what asset allocation is, and what it's not.

Asset allocation is nothing more than a systematic approach to diversification, and comes in two versions: tactical and strategic.

Tactical asset allocators are market-timers in disguise. They base investment decisions on economic and political forecasts, which can be much like looking into a crystal ball. A manager who uses tactical asset allocation typically turns over investments more frequently, which often leads to higher expenses. In turn, the result can be increased volatility—clearly inconsistent with the smoothing effect of portfolio diversification.

Perhaps most importantly, there are no long-term studies which indicate that market timing is worthwhile. In fact, you have to be right at least 75 percent of the time just to break even, after accounting for mistakes and transaction costs.

Strategic asset allocators, on the other hand, place specific percentages in various investment classes, and leave them relatively unchanged. These percentages are chosen based on the investor's long-term needs and risk tolerance. As you approach retirement, for example, you might prefer to minimize your risk and shift from growth to income and/or cash equivalents.

Strategic asset allocation is the age-old concept of sensible diversification where you gain with minimal pain. The goal is to reduce risk more than you reduce investment return. By spreading your money over a wide range of investments such as stocks, bonds, real estate and cash, you maximize return with the least risk. That is, losses in one area are most often offset by gains in another.

For the ten-year period ending December 31, 1989, a diversified portfolio provided investors with a return second only to stocks, with a standard deviation (risk factor) only slightly higher than that of a money market fund. The standard deviation is the degree of volatility one could normally expect from a given asset class. For example, for the ten-year period ending December 31, 1989, money market returns have averaged 9.58%, but in any given year, one could normally expect this rate of return to vary up or down by as much as 3.25%.

Your Options

If you've got the aptitude and time, you can **do your own asset allocation**. In today's world, there is no shortage of financial publications to assist you, including the *Wall Street Journal* and the many newsletters that are full of hands-on advice. The real benefit to this approach is that you can tailor a program to your specific financial needs.

If you elect this method, you must decide whether to place your money in individual stocks or to diversify through a mutual fund. The answer in most cases depends on how much money you plan to invest. If you opt for **individual securities,** the general rule of thumb is that you should own a minimum of 15 stocks in at least 8 different industries to achieve proper diversification. Assuming round lot purchases (100 shares) at an average share price of $40, an investor would need $60,000 to create a diversified stock portfolio!

As a result, many investors have turned to **mutual funds** for liquidity, diversification and professional management. Employing this approach, an investor can diversify across various asset classes with as little as $10,000.

In general, your asset allocation decisions will be driven by **your stage in life.** When you're younger, you may want to emphasize growth-oriented investments like real estate and stocks. As you grow older, bonds and cash should assume greater importance.

Another approach is to invest in **asset allocation funds,** with a professional portfolio manager diversifying your money for you. However, one drawback to this approach is that your asset allocation isn't tailored to your particular financial needs. In effect, the 20-year-old and the 60-year-old investor receive the same asset allocation. In turn, there is no periodic adjustments, based on an individual's changing needs, goals or tolerance for risk.

A third option is to use a **financial planner.** In this case, your assets can be tailored

---

Examples of Asset Allocation: Merrill Lynch Asks Investors to Decide Their Risk Tolerance; Sets Four Asset Allocation Categories

An example of asset allocation was offered in recent news reports of a move by Merrill Lynch & Co., the nation's largest brokerage firm. It will begin asking its 7.2 million retail account investors to decide for themselves their risk tolerance.

It will then place each in one of four risk categories, and its brokers will be instructed to make investment decisions accordingly.

"Conservative for income" is the most cautious approach, and is most often appropriate for retirees. Here the recommended asset allocation is 30% in stocks, 60% in bonds and 10% in cash.

"Conservative for growth" is the next step up in degree of risk. In this category, Merrill Lynch recommends that one's portfolio should be invested 60% in stocks, 30% in bonds and 10% in cash.

"Moderate risk" is the next higher category of risk. Here the recommended asset allocation is 50% in stocks, 40% in bonds and 10% in cash.

"Aggressive Risk" is the highest category of risk-taking. It calls for a portfolio invested 60% in stocks and 40% in bonds.

For comparison, Merrill Lynch's recommended allocation for a balanced corporate pension fund or endowment is 50% in stocks, 45% in bonds and 5% in cash.

to your individual needs. Asset allocation is an integral part of the financial planning process.

Do's and Don'ts

Regardless of which approach you take, here is a list of simple "do's and don'ts" to keep in mind:

1. Do review your asset allocation strategy annually, at a minimum, to assure that it fits your financial goals and objectives.

2. Don't lose faith, should one asset class go through a down cycle. Stay committed. The whole point of diversifying among various asset classes is that each class behaves differently as market conditions change. While this won't necessarily make you rich in the short-run, this will protect the value of your portfolio in the long-term.

3. Do remember that asset allocation means more than simply buying 9 stocks—or 90, for that matter. Even a large portfolio of stocks is relatively undiversified, particularly if you are concentrated in just one sector of the market. The key is to diversify across asset classes—real estate, stocks, bonds and cash.

4. Don't get into market timing, trying to predict the future of the stock, bond and real estate markets. Professional investors with years of experience are rarely able to do it. In fact in the ten-year period ending December 31, 1989, 85% of all money managers failed to outperform the S&P 500 Index.

There you have it. The best way to lower financial risk and maximize returns on a long-term basis is through diversification.

George Ginther, LUTCF, is President of Niagara Financial Services, Inc., Buffalo, New York.

How to Select a Money Manager

by Heidi Steiger

Individuals close to retirement age may find themselves confronted with personal crises that place them in the uncomfortable position of having to manage sums of money larger than any they've ever had before. Consider for instance what an individual might do if faced with either of the following situations:

- An elderly mother who could not care for herself any longer went to live in a nursing home. Not wanting to sign over her assets to the home, she gives the pre-retiree her $700,000 portfolio to manage.

- The breadwinning spouse dies just before retiring after 35 years of work, leaving a $500,000 insurance policy.

As professional pre-retirement planners, you may be called upon to provide financial direction for individuals in dilemmas such as these. One option for these individuals is professional money management, which can help them grow their nest eggs to last through retirement years.

A money manager, for a fee, takes control of an individual's assets and creates and manages an investment portfolio tailored to meet the individual's needs. A money manager provides a more individualized service than insurance company portfolios, bank pooled funds or mutual funds. And since each portfolio is invested individually, it is not affected by the actions of other investors using the same manager.

Today, there are approximately 11,000 money management firms in the U.S.— double the number 5 years ago. These firms range in size from one person firms to huge companies that invest billions of dollars for clients. Not surprisingly, their investment approaches vary. Here's what you need to know to help your clients find the money manager that's right for them.

Finding the Right Money Manager

Since most money managers don't advertise, recommendations from accountants, lawyers or financial planners are a good way to begin a search for a money manager. There are consultants who will screen money managers, suggest several for consideration and evaluate their performance on a client's behalf. Another valuable source might be directories such as the Directory of Registered Investment Advisors and periodicals such as "Pensions & Investments."

Every firm will provide its past performance records, but deciphering them can be difficult. Also, many firms are relatively new and won't have meaningful track records showing performance over a full market cycle of up and down years. The most desirable performance records will include the severe bear market in 1973–1974.

But even when looking at the records of more established firms, the following guidelines should be used in one's analysis:

- Examine the manager's performance relative to a standard index such as the S&P 500.

- Understand how the performance numbers are computed. They're likely to be objective if supplied by a firm whose business is monitoring money managers' performances. If not, carefully question how the data base was established, and make sure the numbers were audited for the entire time period being illustrated.

- Check the data on both a long-term and year-by-year basis. The money manager may start with the year prior to a superior performance year in order to mask average numbers over the next ten.

- Ask questions probing the strengths and weaknesses of each firm's investment style. What conditions will result in mediocre or poor performance? Are these events likely?

- No matter how good the track record, it is unlikely any manager can beat the averages every year. Seven or eight years out of ten is considered to be a good track record.

Selecting a Reliable Financial Planner
Is the Responsibility
of Every Mature Consumer

Seeking honest assistance with financial planning is a challenge facing every mature consumer.

There are legions of honest, competent financial planners who put clients' interests above all else, and who charge reasonably for services rendered.

Unfortunately, the financial planners who tend to make the news are the occasional dishonest or unqualified ones who end up doing more harm than good.

Protecting one's nest egg remains the responsibility of the consumer, and the penalties for carelessness can be severe. An association of state securities law regulators estimated that, in a recent two-year period, fraud and abuse by financial planners cost an estimated 22,000 investors $400 million.

The demand for financial planning is huge, with an estimated 10 million Americans using the services of financial planners. The largest association in the field, the International Association of Financial Planners (IAFP) surveyed its 54,000 members and determined that they controlled or guided the investment of $154 billion of their clients' money in the past year.

There are other associations in the field, as well. Among them: the International Association of Registered Financial Planners and the National Association of Personal Financial Advisors.

Regulatory organizations include the Securities and Exchange Commission (SEC), the federal agency which licenses investment advisers. The SEC has licensed only 14,000 out of about 300,000 individuals who hold themselves out to be financial planners. The SEC does not verify the education or experience of applicants. Licensed advisers are supposed to be inspected an average of every three years; but some of the 14,000 licensed advisers have never been checked by the agency.

The North American Securities Administrators Assn. (NASAA), the state securities law regulators, suggests you check the background of financial planners or other investment professionals with your state's security office. To get the name and telephone number of your state's securities regulation office, call the NASAA office in Washington, D.C. at 202-737-0900.

Before starting a relationship with a financial planner, the client should understand clearly how the consultant will be compensated. Most planners charge a fee for advice, then collect commissions for selling investment and insurance products. A small percent of planners work on a fee-only basis, charging clients for their advice, then leaving clients on their own to seek out investments and insurance. There are also variations, such as fee offsets. This is when the consultant's fee is reduced if commissions are earned when advice is implemented by a client.

People are usually too timid to ask a physician or an attorney about fees. But when it comes to financial planners, it is absolutely essential that mature consumers insist upon complete disclosure and candor from anyone who proposes to handle their investments.

Consistency is important. Chasing the top performer each year will probably yield below-average results, since the winners in up markets tend to take the most risk and are often hurt most when the market turns down.

In addition to setting forth overall objectives, a money manager needs to be apprised of any cash inflows or outflows within the next 12–18 month horizon that could affect investment planning. In addition to impending retirement, these might include any changes in current income or alternative minimum tax payments.

The more the money manager knows about your clients' needs, the better job he or she can do of finding investments to meet their objectives.

How the Relationship Works

Money managers charge an investment advisory fee that can range between 0.75 and 2 percent of the assets under management each year. In addition, there are transaction costs for the trades themselves. The total charges will be between 1 and 3 percent of the assets under management. That means, on a $250,000 portfolio, a fee of $3,750 to a manager whose total charge is 1.5 percent for advisory fees and commissions. Charges are either billed directly or deducted from the portfolio.

Money management firms provide notification of each trade after it occurs. In addition, they send monthly statements listing current holdings at market value. Most firms will also compare the individual portfolio's performance to a standard index, such as the S&P 500.

At least once a year, investors should meet with the firm to review the portfolio and objectives. Some investors may want to confer twice a year, others only every other year. The decision is generally up to the individual, and often depends upon how frequently their financial situation is changing.

Evaluating Performance

The relationship between client and money manager can go wrong for the same reason many other relationships fail—a lack of communication. Typically, if investors are dissatisfied with their money managers' performance it turns out they did not understand what kind of performance to expect, or somewhere along the line they changed their expectations without telling the money manager.

For example, it is not unrealistic to ask a well-run, conservative money management firm to attempt to exceed inflation by 6 percent a year and top the S&P 500 by at least 2 percent after fees. But if the firm is hired to do that, an investor shouldn't be disappointed when another money manager, whose strategy is more daring, turns in a better performance. That firm may be investing at risk levels unacceptable to the particular investor.

Also, keep in mind that a money manager is asking to handle assets on a discretionary basis. He has an overall investment strategy for a portfolio and should be allowed to execute it freely. Although investors will receive statements of all transactions, performance shouldn't be evaluated—either positively or negatively—on a trade-by-trade basis. Rather, performance should be reviewed annually and over a full market cycle that will enable an investor to evaluate how well the money manager does over up, as well as down markets.

If clients maintain a long-term perspective and occasional contact with their money management firms, they should anticipate positive results and a strong relationship.

Heidi S. Steiger is managing director of the Individual Asset Management division of Neuberger & Berman, New York, New York.

A Relationship Built on Trust and Honesty

by Steven S. Shagrin, J.D., C.F.P.

As in any area where large sums of money are involved, the relationship between a client and a financial planner must be based upon trust and honesty.

As a member financial planner, I take several steps to protect the consumer.

As an employee of a major brokerage firm, I comply with a rule called the "know your client" rule, which requires that we inquire about the financial resources of a client and determine suitability for certain investments.

I take this rule to extremes in retirement planning.

The result of an incorrect action based on imprecise information from a client can cause disaster in pursuing long-term needs. I fully examine the anticipated income and expenditures, current investment and insurance structure, tax consequences, and long-term cash flow requirements, both from after-tax and tax-deferred accounts.

I also undertake an exhaustive discussion of risk and reward and help clients determine their appropriate risk and comfort level. Only then do I recommend a course of action for investment restructuring and funds positioning.

With respect to investment selection, I try to perform as complete a due diligence review as I can. This is done by discussing the investment with our in-house departments, the sponsoring company representatives and other seasoned professionals.

I play devil's advocate, attempting to determine answers to questions about what could possibly go wrong, and how the sponsoring company anticipates taking corrective action. Only then would I consider it an appropriate investment for a client.

Finally, I take professional development seriously. I satisfy the continuing education requirements of my various licensee and professional designations, and very often go beyond the hours that are required in order to obtain the most thorough knowledge I can in my area of expertise.

In summary, by knowing and anticipating my client's situation and needs, by understanding the risks and rewards of alternative investments, and by continuing to improve my knowledge in the changing environment of financial and investment planning, I feel that I'm doing everything I can to protect my clients from the "war stories" of the retired consumer.

For consumer protection resources, I suggest the Institute for Certified Financial Planners (ICFP) in Denver, Colorado for names of Certified Financial Planners, and the National Association of Security Dealers (NASD) in New York for investment brokers.

I also suggest that individuals never act in a vacuum, with just one area of planning. As the most important decisions in life are being weighed, it is of utmost importance to involve all planning professionals in determining an ultimate direction, including the investment broker, insurance specialist, accountant, attorney and financial planner. Finally, family members, particularly the spouse, should be aware of any actions contemplated.

Steven S. Shagrin, J.D., C.F.P., is Vice President, Investments at Smith Barney Shearson, Youngstown, Ohio.

A Five Point Plan for Establishing a Relationship with a Financial Adviser

by Lorraine Decker

Having served, all too often, as expert witnesses in New York Stock Exchange arbitration hearings where retired individuals have lost vast sums of money in unsuitable investments, Ken Decker and I have developed a five point recommendation for mature consumers.

1. Know your investment advisors, how they are compensated, their ethics and standards of practice. Check their references and historical results, determine their commitments to continuing education and their time commitment to you, and meet personally with them several times (at least three) before engaging their services.

2. Put your investment instructions and objectives in writing and have both the advisor and the manager of the brokerage firm acknowledge receipt of the instructions.

3. Develop quantifiable written objectives. Avoid such directions and comments as "I'm a risk avoider" or "I want a secure portfolio." Discuss instead specific objectives, such as "I want an 8 percent gross rate of return, after taking into consideration an inflation rate of 4.75 percent." Or: "I want the portfolio liquid, meaning I can have access to my investments with no more than a 1 percent potential loss within a thirty day period."

4. Before making any investment, ask "What can go wrong?" Analyze all potential risks and losses and determine a written strategy for identifying loss potential before it occurs, and how you will minimize the losses when they do occur. For example, based upon the above investment objective, one question you would ask is "What impact would a 3.75 percent inflation rate or a 5.75 percent inflation rate have on my expected rate of return and liquidity?"

5. Before making any financial decision, ask "What should MERIT my attention?" Consider how your mortality (life expectancy) expenditures (current and future), rate of return (current and required), inflation (current and future), and taxes (income and estate) will interact with your financial decisions.

Lorraine Decker is a principal in Decker & Associates, Inc., Houston, Texas.

The Mature Consumer: Avoiding the Widow's Buying Syndrome

by J. Grady Cash, M.Ed., C.F.P.

Preretirement programs should prepare both spouses for retirement. In most families, one person handles all the major financial decisions. The Widow's Buying Syndrome (WBS) occurs when death of that spouse forces the surviving spouse to make financial decisions for the first time, often about hundreds of thousands of dollars. Alone, in an emotional state, and unprepared to assume the role of financial manager, the Widow's Buying Syndrome can be very stressful and potentially disastrous.

This article explains WBS and shows steps to reduce its effects which can easily be incorporated into existing retirement programs.

The Widow's Buying Syndrome may occur when a recent widow must make decisions about her late husband's life insurance proceeds. However, it could be any decision involving money, such as buying a home or a car or an employee who must decide what to do with a lump sum distribution of a retirement plan. Obviously, this syndrome could occur in either spouse; however, I have observed it most often in widows, hence the name Widow's Buying Syndrome (WBS).

Indecision and Worry

In WBS, when faced with an unfamiliar financial decision, the widow agonizes over it and, unable to decide what to do, she puts it off. As time passes, the stress increases until she worries about the decision constantly. It's as if the fear of making a mistake is so great that she is paralyzed into inaction. This stage may last weeks or months, but finally the pressure becomes too great. She must do something, even if it's wrong. The need to eliminate the worry over the decision becomes greater than the consequences of a bad decision.

Impulsive Action

Whether it is conscious or subconscious, this impulse to act is usually very sudden and potentially dangerous, because this state of mind is emotional and highly susceptible to suggestion.

Even trusted family advisers can be left out of the decision-making process. There is a high risk that she will buy impulsively from the next financial planner she talks to. It doesn't matter whether the planner had been contacting her for months or had met her for the first time that day. When asked about the suddenness of their action, a typical widow's reply is "I just had to do something!"

How Salespersons Use the Widow's Buying Syndrome

Although they may not be familiar with the name, most financial planners who work with retirees understand the Widow's Buying Syndrome. In spite of being told no, they just keep calling and calling. "Ready to do something this week, Mrs. Smith? You really should you know."

After a few such calls, the widow begins to think maybe the salesperson is right. What she doesn't know is that this is a proven sales technique. The salesperson who persists in making those calls every few days will eventually be rewarded when the sudden impulse to act occurs. However, sometimes the impulse to act is so strong, the widow buys from someone on the first contact.

In one of the more disastrous cases I observed, Mrs. M. called me wanting to invest $170,000 in life insurance proceeds she had received several weeks earlier. Since it was late Friday afternoon, she made an appointment for Monday morning, but she missed it.

When I called to remind her of her appointment, she told me a friend of her husband called and came by on Saturday and she invested the entire $170,000 with him. Although she had these funds for several weeks, Mrs. M's impulse to act was so great she couldn't wait until our Monday appointment, even though the actual investments couldn't be made until Monday anyway!

Unfortunately, the broker placed her entire savings of $170,000 in only two investments, both of which declined significantly. In less than six months, Mrs. M's impulsive action cost her over $60,000.

On the other hand, the broker was well paid for his Saturday afternoon, earning about $10,000 in commissions. Since the commissions can be so large, and experienced planners are aware of this tendency for widows to act impulsively, even good financial planners may pressure widows to buy, knowing they would lose a large sale if the impulse strikes at the wrong time. Unfortunately, this sales pressure can just increase the situational stress.

How to Avoid WBS

After becoming a financial educator on topics such as Widows Buying Syndrome, I described these symptoms to David Kentsmith, M.D., clinical psychiatrist and author. Together, we developed the following steps to reduce the potentially disastrous effects of WBS.

Rule #1: Protect yourself from an emotional decision.

Dr. Kentsmith advises that recent widows are very susceptible to emotional decisions. Adhering to a set procedure, such as the following rules, can replace these emotional factors with logic.

Rule #2: Don't make immediate decisions. Let your life return to a normal routine first.

Most experts recommend waiting six months after the death of a spouse before making any major financial decisions. Widows should use that time to educate themselves about finances and to identify qualified experts to help them.

Rule #3: Obtain UNBIASED, professional advice.

According to Dr. Kentsmith, a charismatic or emotional sales presentation can be very powerful on people in this highly suggestive state of mind. Thus, widows should avoid financial planners who sell products. Commission-only planners seldom recommend products they cannot sell and may omit superior alternatives. Because the commissions can be so large, this conflict of interest also exists in fee-plus-commission planners, I recommend the widow hire a fee-only advisor.

If this is not practical, then I recommend working with a fee-plus-commission planner on an hourly basis with the understanding that no products will be purchased through the planner, while adhering to the next rule.

Rule #4: Get a second opinion.

Even if there is no sales bias, no one has a crystal ball. Get a second or even a third opinion. Just go to another expert and say: "This is what someone else has recommended I do. What is your opinion?" When advisors agree, it will help reduce the stress of the decision. If they disagree, the second opinion can help prevent mistakes by giving a different perspective.

Rule #5: Break down big decisions into several little ones.

There is often an all-or-nothing tendency about investing. Dr. Kentsmith points out that one of the best ways to learn is to start by making small decisions and get involved. In finances, this means investing only a small portion of the overall funds. Watch the results and learn from that experience before investing more.

Addressing WBS in Retirement Programs

As preretirement counselors, we should be especially aware of the Widow's Buying Syndrome, since it can occur in anyone facing an unfamiliar financial decision.

Employees who receive lump sum distributions upon retirement can experience similar stress, since that is also an unfamiliar situation. WBS and how to handle it can easily be incorporated into most preretirement planning programs in a few minutes, or addressed directly in a special block on financial planning for the nonfinancial spouse.

If you can prevent one tragedy like Mrs. M's, or an ill-advised investment of a retirement plan distribution, it could be the single most important change you could make in your existing retirement program.

J. Grady Cash, M.Ed., C.F.P., is a principal of Financial Wellness, Omaha, Nebraska.

A Legal Primer on Money Management in Retirement and Legal Options to Cover the Cost of Health Care

by Ellice Fatoullah, J.D.

It costs a lot to get sick in America. Fortunately, for most Americans, the spiraling cost of health care is not an immediate concern as they are either healthy or well-insured. But, for the more than 25 million Americans with no health insurance, and for the countless others with inadequate coverage, the high cost of getting sick poses an ever-present threat of impending pauperization.

Perhaps the most severely under-insured group in the nation are elderly and disabled

persons—and their families—in need of long-term care. In the New York City area, for example, nursing home care averages $50,000 per year. Home care often costs as much as $25,000 per year. Nursing home benefits under Medicare, the health insurance program for the elderly and disabled, are, for all practical purposes, nonexistent.

Thus, elderly couples faced with the prospect of nursing home care for one spouse, or families with a disabled member in need of home care, must finance the costs of such care largely out of their own pockets. For elderly couples this potentially means depleting their life savings and, far too often, impoverishing the spouse who remains at home.

One source of third-party coverage for nursing home care, and an important source of coverage for home care, is Medicaid, the joint federal-state health program for the poor and the medically indigent. But, by definition, to qualify for Medicaid, the applicant must be poor. Thus, an elderly or disabled patient may be required to deplete his or her life savings, and perhaps those of his family and suffer the indignity of poverty before the government will come to his or her aid.

Prompt attention to financial planning and money management, however, can prevent enormous medical costs from devouring an elderly couple's or a family's assets and rendering them virtually bankrupt.

The strategies outlined below involve a multitude of considerations and the most appropriate course for any particular couple or family will depend, in great measure, on the unique facts of the case. Thus, all persons are advised to consult an attorney prior to selecting one or more of the options set forth below.

Money Management and Capacity

For most elderly and disabled persons and their families, an issue of major concern is capacity—how to manage a person's affairs when, and if, that person becomes unable to manage his or her own affairs due to physical or mental illness.

All too often, families assume that, prior to the actual, irreversible onset of incapacity, little or nothing can be done to protect assets and prepare for incapacity. To the contrary, prudent and timely attention

to such issues can assure sound money management and provision of care while simultaneously easing the financial burden of uninsured health care on the spouse and family.

Outright Gifts

The easiest and least costly means of money management for a patient at risk of suffering from a deteriorating capacity is the **outright gift** from the patient to his or her spouse or children. The gift relieves the patient of the burden of managing the assets and the spouse or child assumes this responsibility and seeks to preserve and use the assets for the benefit of the patient. This course is generally recommended for patients with less than $50,000 in assets and can be pursued in a manner which takes full advantage of various federal and state gift tax exemptions.

Outright gifts, however, are not without several drawbacks and risks. First, the spouse or child in receipt of the assets must pay taxes on the income earned by the assets. Second, because there are no formal controls on the use of the funds, the recipient may mismanage or divert the funds. Lastly, and most significantly, because the transferred assets will be in the name of the recipient, and not the patient, they may be reached by the recipient's creditors and, upon the death of the recipient, will be distributed accordingly to the latter's will, thus depriving the patient of the benefit of the funds.

A modification of the outright gift option is to transfer funds or securities into **joint or triple ownership accounts.** This will be considered a gift of the proportionate amount transferred—but the patient will still have the funds in his or her name as well.

Power of Attorney

A second money management option is the **durable power of attorney** (POA), a device whereby the patient nominates another person or persons (usually a family member) to act on his or her behalf.

A POA is "durable" when it specifically states that it continues in effect after the onset of incapacity or incompetency. The standard POA gives the nominee(s) the authority to act on the patient's behalf in a wide range of financial matters and special language may be drafted to broaden this authority to include decisions relating to government benefits such as Medicare and Medicaid and pensions. Under a durable POA, the nominee(s) may manage the patient's financial affairs both prior to and during the incapacity.

A POA is a convenient device because it is relatively simple to draft and execute and is revocable by the patient at any time prior to the onset of incapacity. The disadvantages of POA are that POAs are still often not recognized by banks, brokerage houses and insurance companies unless executed specifically for that institution. Also, by itself, a POA does nothing to protect the patient's assets from the ravages of high health care costs.

Conservatorship

Perhaps the most drastic, and certainly the least desirable money management option is **conservatorship.**

A conservatorship is a judicial proceeding whereby a court appoints a "conservator" (usually a family member or friend) to care for the property of the patient, the "conservatee," upon a finding that the latter, due to advanced illness, age, etc., is unable to manage his or her own financial affairs. One advantage of this alternative is that, unlike an outright gift or POA, the court supervises the conservator's management of the assets to ensure that the conservatee's needs are being met.

In many instances a conservatorship may be the only practical option to negotiate

stocks or transfer funds if the patient is truly and completely lacking the mental capacity to make legal decisions.

A conservatorship, however, has several distinct disadvantages that render it an option of last resort. First, it involves a formal court proceeding to assess the capacity and needs of the proposed conservatee. As a result, a family seeking a conservatorship will incur both legal and medical expert fees.

Second, the proceeding itself is time consuming and may take several months to complete, potentially leaving a patient's financial affairs in a state of flux. Finally, because a conservatorship is designed to preserve the assets of the conservatee, other prudent estate and tax planning strategies such as gifts to children or trust funds and Medicaid eligibility may be precluded.

Trusts

By far, the most desirable money management tool for elderly and disabled persons with sufficient assets is **trust**. Indeed, it is highly recommended for estates in excess of $100,000 and for persons of seventy-five years of age and older. (For lesser estates or younger persons, a trust may also be appropriate or, alternatively, a gift or POA or some combination thereof, depending on the family's circumstances and wishes.)

A trust is an agreement between the **"grantor,"** the person who transfers assets into the trust, and the **"trustee,"** the recipient of the assets, whereby the trustee agrees to manage and use the trust assets in accordance with the terms of the trust agreement. The trust is a very flexible device which can guarantee that the grantor will be adequately provided for while simultaneously taking advantage of sound estate planning techniques and, possibly, government entitlements such as Medicaid. (Although with the enactment of the Consolidated Budget Reconciliation Act of 1986, "COBRA", certain "Medical qualifying trusts" will be disqualified for assistance.

Also, trusts are widely recognized by banks, insurance companies and brokerage houses, enabling the assets to be easily managed. A significant advantage of trusts is that, ordinarily, their terms provide for the distribution of the assets at the end of the trust term, generally upon the death of the grantor. This procedure can avoid the expensive and lengthy process of probating a will.

Lastly, because the trust assets may belong to the trust and not the trustee, the latter may not pay any taxes or income earned by the trust assets, unlike the recipient of an outright gift.

Like all money management options, however, trusts are not without drawbacks and risks warranting special attention. Most importantly, the trustee must be someone the patient or grantor has complete confidence in, as often the trust terms that offer the most protection give the trustee the greatest discretion in managing and using the assets.

In addition, a trust is somewhat more burdensome than an outright gift or POA. The family will incur legal fees to establish the trust and the trustee (again, usually a family member or friend) will assume administrative responsibilities such as filing an annual tax return.

Wills

It goes without saying that everyone should have a **will**. But, spouses of elderly persons in need of long-term care and the parents of disabled children may require special will provisions to provide for the care of their loved one upon their death or to guarantee the preservation of their assets for other heirs.

Under the law of most states, surviving spouses have an absolute right to an **"elective share."** That is, even if a person's will leaves nothing to the surviving spouse, the latter has a right to take one-third, if there are children, or one-half, if there are no children, of the deceased spouse's estate. The purpose of this law is to ensure that the surviving spouse is not left without any means of support.

If the surviving spouse is in a nursing home and already receiving Medicaid benefits, his or her elective share will simply go toward the cost of the nursing home, which Medicaid would otherwise pay. Thus, under these circumstances, the surviving spouse receives no marginal benefit from the elective share and the only result is to reduce the inheritance of the other heirs who are, of course, usually the children. This result can be avoided, however, through appropriately drafted will provisions which comply with the statutory elective share requirement while also preserving the assets for the other heirs.

For parents of disabled children, an important concern in drafting a will is how to provide for the needs of their disabled child upon their death. They seek to guarantee that the routine support needs of their child are met without exhausting the assets on the high cost of medical care.

Fortunately, such a result can be obtained by including a special trust provision for the disabled child in the will. This trust can meet the child's support needs without jeopardizing his or her eligibility for Medicaid to cover the cost of medical care.

Conclusion

Many of these options may be used in conjunction with each other. For example, an elderly person should always execute a Power of Attorney although it should not be relied upon exclusively. Also a trust in conjunction with a triple joint bank account and a partial outright gift may protect the disabled family member and also provide the greatest flexibility.

Medicare, Medicaid and Private Insurance

The astronomical costs of long-term care virtually guarantee that, at some point, the middle-income patient or his or her family will have to turn to government benefit options for assistance in financing such costs. Consequently, it is crucial that the patient and his or her spouse and family understand the important differences between Medicare and Medicaid and their rights under both programs.

Medicare

Medicare is the federal health insurance program for the elderly and disabled and is linked with the Social Security system. Over 95% of Americans over the age of sixty-five, and many disabled persons, are entitled to receive Medicare benefits because of their contributions to the Social Security system.

In other words, Medicare, unlike Medicaid, does not have any income eligibility requirements; all individuals receive the same benefits regardless of their wealth.

But, as most elderly and disabled beneficiaries soon discover, Medicare does not cover many medical costs. In fact, Medicare covers less than one-half (44%) of the cost of the average elderly person's medical care. The elderly person must finance the remaining 56% out of his or her own pocket, through a supplemental "Medigap" insurance policy, or by qualifying for Medicaid.

Medicare is divided into two parts, "A" and "B." Part A is the **hospital insurance** program and covers the first 60 days of hospital care in a given year, less an annual deductible, currently $540. Part A benefits also will pay for an additional 30 days per year, less a $135 per day deductible. Finally,

part A includes 60 "lifetime reserve" days of hospital care with a deductible of $270 per day.

Part B, which the patient may enroll in for a monthly premium of $24.80, covers 80% of the "reasonable costs" of **physician** and other services, less an annual deductible of $75.

Be advised, however, that many physicians do not accept the Medicare rate as payment in full and may charge the patient more than the 20% of the fee not covered by Medicare.

Significantly, however, Medicare provides little coverage for **nursing home** care. Under current rules, Medicare pays the costs of up to 100 days in a skilled nursing facility but will not pay for custodial nursing home care, the service in greatest demand by elderly and disabled patients.

Medigap Insurance Policies

As mentioned previously, Medicare pays for only 44% of the average health care bill, leaving the consumer to pay the remainder out of his or her pocket, or to find a comprehensive **"Medigap"** policy. Unfortunately, virtually all Medigap policies fail to fill in the gaps.

For example, take a hypothetical $10,000 hip operation. Medicare pays for only 80% of Medicare's usual and customary charge. Medicare's usual and customary charge would be, hypothetically, $6,000. Therefore, Medicare would pay only $4,800 (80% of $6,000 = $4,800) on the $10,000 actually charged by the physician.

A traditional Medigap policy will pay the 20% differential between $4,800 + $6,000— but not the $4,000 difference between Medicare's usual and customary and the physician's actual charge.

Sadly, the elderly consumer burned once with an enormous copayment will then seek to purchase additional Medigap policies. Unfortunately, these policies often duplicate each other without extending coverage.

For most elderly consumers the best option is to obtain a Medigap policy that pays 80–100% of the amount actually charged by the physician. Under some policies, 100% of the physician's fee will be reimbursed, private rooms are covered, and it is guaranteed renewable for life. Such policies do have a fairly stringent pre-existing illness requirement in that it will not cover illnesses treated 180 days prior to coverage and there is a 60 day waiting period for other preexisting illness after coverage commences.

Under other policies, preexisting conditions are covered after 90 days. It is also guaranteed renewable for life, and it pays up to 150% of Medicare's approved rate. Policies also pay for a private room.

Medicaid

Medicaid is the health care program for the poor and medically indigent, jointly financed by federal, state and local governments and administered by local Departments of Social Services. To qualify for Medicaid, the applicant or patient must meet certain income and resource eligibility requirements. For example, in New York State, the income level for single persons is $454 per month and for couples, $645 per month.

(It should be stressed, however, that a person or couple whose income exceeds these levels will nevertheless still qualify for Medicaid if their health care costs exceed their income for a given period. This is known as the **"spend down"** provision.) The resource level in New York State for an individual is $3,100 and for a couple, $4,750.

Resources may include bank accounts, stocks and bonds or other property with an aggregate value equal to or less than the applicable resource level. In addition, each individual is entitled to a special burial fund of $1,500.

Finally, a **home** is defined as an **"exempt resource,"** and ownership of a home will not render a person ineligible for Medicaid if the person or his or her spouse actually resides in the home.

The most important thing to bear in mind regarding Medicaid eligibility is that a person cannot simply **transfer his or her assets** and, when left with only the applicable level of resources, apply for Medicaid.

Under both state and federal law, Medicaid will be denied for two years from the date of the transfer if the applicant has transferred $12,000 or less in assets within two years of the date of application.

If the amount transferred was in excess of $12,000, Medicaid will be denied for two years plus an additional month from the date of the transfer for each $2,000 in excess of $12,000. An applicant who has transferred funds in this manner can qualify for Medicaid sooner only if he or she can prove that the transfer was exclusively for some purpose other than qualifying for Medicaid or if he or she incurs medical expenses equal to or greater than the amount transferred.

In effect, the laws on transfers of assets create a two-year waiting period before a person who has made such transfers can apply for Medicaid. The above transfer rules are in effect now. However, states have the discretion to implement new transfer rules for all transfers made on or after July 1, 1988.

One planning technique often employed was to transfer assets into a trust but still have the funds available for the benefit of the grantor or the grantor's spouse. Unfortunately, pursuant to the Consolidated Budget Reconciliation Act (COBRA), P.L. 99-272 of 1986, this option has been foreclosed.

The statute defines a **"Medicaid qualifying trust"** and then treats funds placed into this sort of a trust as still belonging to the grantor, as if no transfer had occurred. Many kinds of trusts, however, may still be written that would not disqualify the patient from Medicaid.

An issue of great concern for elderly couples, and an area where there is much misunderstanding and misinformation, is whether the spouse who remains at home (the "**community spouse**") must, in effect, pauperize himself or herself in order for the patient spouse to qualify for Medicaid.

The answer to this concern is an emphatic "NO!" When an elderly spouse requires long-term care, only that spouse need apply for Medicaid. This will change for all patients institutionalized on or after September 30, 1989.

There is no requirement that, if one spouse needs Medicaid, then both spouses must apply. Indeed, under the federal Consent Decree signed in the case of *Brill v. Perales,* the income and resources of the community spouse can be considered as available to pay the cost of the patient spouse's care only during the first full calendar month in which institutionalization occurs, unless the spouse at home voluntarily applies for and is eligible for Medicaid.

In the latter situation, the resources, but not the income, of the community spouse will be considered available to pay for the patient spouse's care only for the first six months following the institutionalization.

The Medicaid agency may nonetheless ask the community spouse for a contribution toward the cost of the patient spouse's care. If however, the community spouse cannot afford to make the requested contribution, he or she may refuse to do so under Social Services Law section 366.3(a) and, despite such refusal, Medicaid must still be provided for the patient spouse. In accordance with the Brill Consent Decree, hospitals, nursing homes and Medicaid offices must advise all long-term care Medicaid applicants that the community spouse has the right to refuse to contribute income

and resources if the community spouse needs the funds for his or her own support.

The Brill case has thus corrected the former Medicaid practice of soliciting a contribution from community spouses without informing them of their right not to contribute.

Private Nursing Home Insurance

There is private insurance to pay for nursing home care. Unfortunately, however, under even the most recommended policies, the patient must be diagnosed as medically requiring "**skilled nursing facility**" care upon entrance to the facility. This may cause substantial denials of coverage as formal "**skilled nursing care**" is a stringent standard that many patients needing custodial care would not meet.

Personal Management and Health Care Decisions

Fifteen states do not have **living will** legislation. A living will is an advance directive asking that treatment be withheld or withdrawn when the treatment would merely prolong the dying process. Under the In Re Fox case, the New York State Court of Appeals upheld the right of an individual to have life sustaining treatment withheld when, in advance, the individual stated clearly his desire to do so. In that case the individual was a priest and he made his advance directives, orally, to a group of priests.

Unless you are in the unlikely situation of making your advance directive to a group of priests, then you should write your directives down in the firm of a living will. Although not recognized by statute in New York State, a written living will would meet the In Re Fox standards of "clear and convincing evidence."

In August of 1987, New York State enacted the nation's first Do Not Resuscitate (DNR) statute. This statute retains the legal presumption in favor of resuscitating a patient, but it also provides that the patient with capacity may consent in advance to a DNR order. The statute also designates surrogate decision makers to approve such orders for patients who lack the capacity to make the decision on their own, and it provides special rules for decisions on behalf of minors and mentally ill patients. This DNR bill only applies to persons in terminally ill conditions.

A living will can also be written if an individual is desirous of not living in an irreversible, vegetative state which is not necessarily terminal. Unfortunately, there is about to be a great deal of litigation around this issue as nursing homes are refusing to honor patients' or families' wishes to withhold life sustaining treatment or feeding tubes.

In at least 50% of these cases, however, litigation can be avoided. For example, hospitals are much more likely to honor living will declarations than nursing homes and simply moving the patient to a hospital where the living will declaration would be recognized could avoid the law suit. Under certain circumstances, however, judicial enforcement of a living will declaration may be necessary.

Ms. Fatoullah, J.D., is an attorney with Fatoullah Associates, New York, New York.

4

INSURANCE TOPICS

Insurance: A Confusing, Expensive Item for the Mature Consumer

by L. Malcolm Rodman

A significant part of any mature individual's or family's budget goes to pay insurance premiums. Not only is insurance a costly item, and becoming more so, it is also a bewildering area of complicated policies and overly-enthusiastic salesmen.

Advising mature consumers on being knowledgeable purchasers of insurance is likewise a complicated job. The challenges fall into the following areas:

1. For those over age 65, how to purchase so-called medigap insurance to supplement benefits paid by the Medicare program?
2. For everyone: how to insure against catastrophic illness and long-term nursing home care, at affordable premiums?
3. For those employed and those retired: what to do when rising insurance premiums force employers to shift health insurance costs to workers or pensioners?
4. What steps, if any, should an annuity holder take in the face of a failing insurer?

Consumers can turn to trusted insurance agents, so long as they realize agents live on sales commissions. Also, many senior advocacy organizations, such as AARP, have a substantial financial interest in selling insurance products.

More objective are local government consumer protection agencies and state insurance commissions. However, these agencies frequently are over-worked and a consumer has difficulty getting individual questions answered.

Some non-profit consumer groups, such as the Washington, D.C.-based United Seniors Health Cooperative, sell no products and specialize in dispensing impartial advice through news releases and publications. To inquire about their offerings, retirement planners can contact them at 1331 H Street, N.W., Suite 500, Washington, D.C. 20005; or telephone 202-393-6222.

Committees of the U.S. Congress, spurred by AARP and others, have held repeated hearings which publicize abuses in selling insurance policies to the elderly, and in possible legislative solutions.

One outcome of these hearings are the checklists which consumers can utilize in shopping for medigap and nursing home policies.

More basic was legislation enacted late in 1990 which mandates state regulators and the insurance industry totally reform the medigap insurance field by mid-1992.

The state insurance commissioners to date have designed 10 standardized policies to replace thousands of so-called medigap policies now on the market. They propose a range of policies which all contain a core of benefits, such as: payment of the patient's 20% share of doctors' bills; payment of the patient's $157-per-day contribution to hospital bills for the 61st through 90th day of hospital confinement and some coverage for hospital stays beyond 90 days.

Senate Aging Committee's Tips on Purchasing
Medicare Supplemental (Medigap) Health Insurance

1. Identify Medicare's gaps to determine what is important to you in a Medigap policy. Also consider such policy feature as premiums, waiting periods, pre-existing condition exclusions and maximum benefit clauses.
2. Take into account any other coverage you have that continues beyond age 65.
3. Consider how much you can afford to pay out of your own pocket for hospital and medical bills, as opposed to how much you can afford to pay for premiums.
4. Find out which doctors accept Medicare assignment and are participating physicians, from your local Social Security office or Area Agency on Aging.
5. Work with hometown insurance agents and companies you know.
6. Ask your friends if they've had good claims experience with their Medigap policies.
7. Investigate group insurance sold by legitimate organizations and associations.
8. Purchase one good comprehensive Medigap policy to avoid overlaps.
9. Be careful before giving up an existing policy and taking out a new one.
10. Beware of policies that let the insurer refuse to renew your policy on an individual basis.
11. Remember no Medigap policy is issued or guaranteed by state or federal government.
12. Do not pay cash for insurance—write a check or money order payable to the company, not the agent. Pay only a deposit, not a full annual premium, until you have received the policy.
13. Keep handy the agent and company's name, address and telephone number.
14. Remember: any agent trying to sell a Medigap policy that duplicates either your Medicare coverage or any private insurance you have may be subject to criminal penalties. It is also illegal for anyone to pretend to be from Medicare or any government agency.
15. Medicare supplement policies issued after 1980 must meet minimum standards, concerning pre-existing conditions, a 30-day free look period, and a payout of 60 to 64 percent of all premiums collected as benefits. Such standards do not apply to policies covering long-term care, hospital indemnity policies or dread disease policies.

Senate Aging Committee's Tips on Purchasing
Long Term Care (Nursing Home) Insurance

1. Determine the level of care the policy covers—skilled care, intermediate care and/or custodial care. Make sure the policy covers the levels of care you want.
2. Make sure the policy provides inflation protection for the daily coverage rate.
3. Know how long the policy will provide benefits. For a chronic condition and a stay of more than 3 months, the average length of stay is 2.5 years.
4. Do not buy policies with a requirement for prior hospitalization.
5. Avoid policies with a period of confinement of more than 90 days.
6. If you choose a policy with a waiting period, be sure you understand how much out-of-pocket costs you will incur before coverage begins.
7. Review the cost implications of an elimination period. The longer the elimination period, the less expensive the premium.
8. Be aware of your policy's exclusions. Some do not cover Parkinson's or Alzheimer's diseases.
9. Remember, most policies do not require the policy holder to continue to pay premiums while confined to a nursing home.
10. Most policies are not sold to persons over a certain age, usually 80 or 85. Try to avoid a policy that states premiums will go up with attained age.
11. Avoid policies not "guaranteed renewable for life."
12. Be truthful when answering questions from insurers. Information withheld or falsified by you might jeopardize future claims or cause a policy to be cancelled.

Various options go beyond the basic core package of services, at added premium cost. Now, private insurers must decide how many of the ten plans private insurers will offer, and at what premium costs.

Annuity holders face new problems revolving around the solvency of insurance companies which issue them. This is a worry unknown to previous generations of annuitants. It is an outgrowth of some insurers' investment policies of the past decade plus the pension management practices of some corporations which have shifted pension funds into GICs—guaranteed investment contracts.

GICs fall outside the pension plan protection of the government's Pension Benefit Guarantee Corporation. Thus, if an insurer issuing GICs fails, it threatens the future annuity income of tens of thousands of retirees.

Most policyholders are protected by state insurance guarantee funds. Only residents of Louisiana and the District of Columbia have no such protection.

Consumers have been advised by many experts not to panic and attempt to cash in annuities prematurely. For one thing, there are penalties for terminating annuities during the early years of their life. Since they are tax-deferred investment vehicles, the owner must roll them over into similar instruments or face stiff tax penalties. There are new sales commissions and fees to pay. Also, once an annuity policy has begun paying benefits, it cannot generally be cancelled.

Mr. Rodman is Editor of Retirement Planning.

Buyers Must Beware of Confusing Terms in Long Term Care Policies

by Dale M. Larson

One of the most significant issues facing Americans in the next decade is financing the cost of long term health care. It is estimated that at least one of every four Americans over age 65 will eventually enter a nursing home, and more will need long term care at home. Increasing life expectancy and an exploding elderly population are combining to create a demand/financing crisis of staggering proportions.

Middle-income elderly are seeing a lifetime of savings wiped out. Medicare only covers short term post hospital convalescence and Medicaid, the long term care financing option of last resort for those who are or become impoverished, is in danger of collapsing under the strain of increasing demand in the face of budgetary realities.

Government leaders and astute specialists in aging have recognized that a significant part of the solution to this crisis is private long term care insurance. State and Federal government officials are beginning to actively promote this idea and new private long term care insurance programs are appearing regularly. Unfortunately, there is a wide divergence in the quality of available long term care policies and in the range of services covered.

Because of this divergence and the fact that language and terms used in such policies can be confusing, purchasers of long term care insurance need to be cautious and discerning. Many will turn to financial planners. Unfortunately, most of these professionals are not familiar with the critical issues of evaluating long term care insurance.

One of the most important issues is what kind of coverage is provided for custodial care. Some programs do not cover custodial care at all (this is often noted in the list of Exclusions). Some programs, while offering reasonable or even substantial benefits for skilled nursing care (and in some cases intermediate care), offer greatly reduced payments, reduced length of coverage, increased elimination periods, or a combination of any or all of the above. Many of these plans may also require anywhere from 3 to 20 days of skilled (or intermediate) nursing care before custodial care will be covered. This can effectively eliminate the custodial care benefit, since skilled care often may not last that long. The best plans make no distinction in coverage for different levels of care.

Another significant issue is whether the policy provides coverage for organically based mental or nervous disorders. An unqualified blanket exclusion of all mental or nervous disorders means that the company would not be required to cover such common causes of nursing home confinement as Alzheimer's Disease, and other forms of senility, Parkinson's Disease, ALS, MS, etc.

The best plans cover organically based mental and nervous disorders.

Home care coverage is perhaps the most divergent and confusing area of long term care insurance. Because of the consumer demand for home care coverage, most new plans offer some form of home care benefits. Because of the greater likelihood of utilization of home care services and the lack of significant meaningful actuarial data on such utilization, insurance companies have placed various limits on their home care benefits. For example coverage may be limited to only certain services, such as care by a registered nurse (i.e., skilled care); it may pay less and/or more for a shorter period of time that would be paid for nursing home care; it may require a minimum period of prior nursing home and/or hospital confinement; or have a combination or any or all of the above restrictions. Although consumers would like it to be otherwise, insurers are not interested in paying out more to care for policy holders at home than it would cost to care for them in a nursing home.

Consumers need to consider the realistic benefits not the theoretical benefits. For example, a plan may offer to pay for several years of home care that requires a nurse. However, it is unlikely that a person would actually require care by a nurse for more than a few months, at most, without either getting well or deteriorating in health to a point where care in a nursing home would be more economical.

Most policies require a prior hospital stay of three days to be eligible for long term care benefits. The purpose of this requirement is to prevent unnecessary or discretionary use of benefits (which is contrary to the fundamental principle of insurance, i.e., the insured event be random). Although objections can be raised to this requirement, so far the alternatives to its use have

Beware of Insurance Agents Using "Scare" Tactics

Both Congress and its investigative arm, the General Accounting Office, have expressed alarm over nursing home and long-term care insurance policies which are full of exclusions, making them almost useless to protect the elderly.

You must caution your clientele against hasty purchases of this important insurance protection, especially from overeager or fast-talking salesmen.

The GAO said its study showed that 420,000 people have such policies, offered by at least 25 companies. Premiums ranged from $20 to $7,030, depending on age and coverage.

Also, check to see if your state has adopted a model law, forbidding exclusions of Alzheimer's, prohibiting cancellation of policies solely for age and providing other protections.

been either substantially higher premiums or requirements which can prove even more restrictive than the three day hospitalization. An objective care/case management system could replace this requirement in the future. But adequate widespread care management does not currently exist.

Some plans will only pay for care in skilled nursing facilities. The better plans pay in any licensed nursing home.

Most plans will not cover preexisting health conditions until a certain period (typically 90 or 180 days) of time after the policy takes effect. Some plans may waiver (i.e., exclude from coverage) certain preexisting conditions either temporarily or permanently. Consumers should be wary about accepting plans which waiver their health problems. Also, certain health problems may make a person uninsurable or only able to obtain certain types of limited coverage.

Many plans offer a choice of elimination periods. An elimination period is a period of time, e.g., 0, 20, or 100 days, at the beginning of covered services for which no benefits are payable. It is like a deductible. The longer the elimination period, the lower the premium.

Some plans are conditionally renewable, which means that the company has the right to cancel the coverage if it does so for all holders of like policies in a state. Guaranteed renewable life plans are better because they cannot be cancelled under any circumstances (except for non-payment of premium). However the guarantee is only as good as the company behind it. Wise consumers should avoid any plan which cancels or terminates at a certain age. (Typically the age when coverage is most likely to be needed.) All plans reserve the right to change the table rates on a statewide basis.

The cost of long term insurance depends on a wide number of variables, such as age at application (some plans may not accept applicants above a certain age), the amount and types of benefits, the length of coverage, the elimination period, health (in some cases), etc. Generally speaking, all other things being equal, the younger and healthier an applicant is, the lower the premium. Most policies do not increase the premiums for existing policy-holders due to advancing age or changes in health, although some do increase premiums with age. Some plans may also waive premium payments after a certain period of paid benefits.

Remember that cost is only one component of value. If the plan does not provide coverage adequate to meet a person's needs, it is of no value no matter how little it costs.

Finally, everyone's needs are different. There is no one plan that is best for everyone. The wise shopper will look at several plans to find the one that best fits his or her needs. Consumers and their advisors need to evaluate carefully the types of services they want covered. Policies which cover both nursing home and home care are more expensive than those covering nursing home care alone. While a plan covering only home care may be emotionally attractive, appealing to the feeling of wanting to avoid institutionalization, the fact is that, in many cases, a nursing home stay is ultimately unavoidable. Given the potentially catastrophic financial consequences of a long stay in a nursing home, purchasing a home care only plan could leave a person with a false sense of security while leaving them vulnerable to financial disaster. Even better is to utilize the services of a specialist in long term care insurance who has access to a wide variety of quality plans. This trained professional can guide the shopper through the often confusing maze of varying features and help the consumer find the plan that best fits his or her needs.

Many plans pay a pre-agreed fixed daily amount (indemnity) for covered services although a few pay a percentage of actual costs. Purchasers of indemnity type plans need to evaluate their ability to pay any portion of anticipated costs and buy an indemnity amount large enough to pay the remaining portion. It is also wise to allow a cushion for inflation unless the plan has an automatic benefit increase feature.

Mr. Larson is Executive Vice President of LTC, Inc., Bellevue, Washington.

Experts Offer a Buyers' Guide to Long Term Care Policies

by Shirley and John Hanson

In our consumers' guide to long term care insurance, we offer the following clues in shopping for a policy to meet an individual's specific circumstances:

Does the policy cover long term care?

Long term nursing home care, especially custodial care, is not covered by Medicare or Medicare Supplement policies.

LOOK FOR: A special insurance policy specifically designed to cover long term care.

LOOK OUT FOR: Policies that will only pay on "Medicare approved charges" or that will only pay in a "skilled facility certified by Medicare."

What is the "rating" of the insurance company?

The A.M. Best Company, independent analysts of the insurance industry, analyzes both the financial strength and the operating performance of insurance companies, and then assigns a "rating" based on their findings. The ratings are classified as follows:

A+ Superior   A Excellent
B+ Very Good   B Good
C+ Fair   C Poor

The "rating" of an insurance company can be found by asking the agent for a copy of the A.M. Best Report, or contacting your local library, which usually has an A.M. Best Directory.

LOOK FOR: Companies that have an A+ or A Rating.

LOOK OUT FOR: Companies that have no A.M. Best Rating or that have a low rating (C+ or C).

What is the renewability of the policy?

LOOK FOR: Policies which are "Guaranteed Renewable for Life" (can only be cancelled by the Company due to non-payment of premiums).

LOOK OUT FOR: Policies that can be cancelled by the Company: due to the policyholder's age, health, number of claims; or, if all such policies are cancelled, on a "statewide" or "group" basis. These policies offer the least permanent protection.

What levels of nursing care are covered?

LOOK FOR: A policy that pays full benefits for all levels of nursing are (Skilled, Intermediate, and Custodial) provided in a licensed nursing facility.

LOOK OUT FOR: Policies which cover only skilled nursing care; policies which require the patient to have skilled nursing care before paying any benefits for custodial care, or policies that pay long term benefits only for skilled nursing care, and short term or reduced benefits for custodial care.

What types of nursing facilities are covered?

LOOK FOR: A policy which pays for confinement in any state licensed nursing facility.

LOOK OUT FOR: Policies which require the patient to be confined in a "skilled nursing facility" or require that the nursing facility be "certified by Medicare." (Most nursing facilities in the U.S. are not skilled nursing facilities and most nursing facilities are not certified by Medicare.)

Do premiums increase with age?

LOOK FOR: Policies whose premiums do not increase with age. (Rates are "locked in" at entry age rate.)

LOOK OUT FOR: Policies whose premium increases with age. A policy that is purchased today at a reasonable rate may be too expensive in the future if the premium increases as age increases (and as one's risk due to age and health increases), causing many people to "drop" needed protection.

Pre-existing conditions.

LOOK FOR: A policy which will cover pre-existing conditions (usually after the policy has been in effect for six months or less).

LOOK OUT FOR: Policies which do not cover pre-existing conditions or which impose long waiting periods (such as one year or more).

Exclusions.

LOOK FOR: Policies which cover senility, Alzheimer's disease and other organic brain diseases. (A large percentage of long term nursing home confinements are due to these conditions.)

LOOK OUT FOR: Policies which exclude confinements due to Alzheimer's disease, senility and related conditions. (These policies may be worded so that they "will not pay for any confinement due to mental or nervous disorders.")

Choice of options.

LOOK FOR: Policies which offer you a choice of options (see below), with a wide range of premium amounts, according to your needs and budget:

Various elimination periods, often called "deductibles," (i.e., 20-day elimination period, 100 day elimination period).

Various daily benefit amounts (i.e., $40/day, $60/day, $80/day).

Various lengths of paid confinement (i.e., 4 years, 6 years, etc., of nursing home confinement).

LOOK OUT FOR: Policies which offer very few options and/or which have such high premium rates that they are not affordable.

Special Features:

Some policies are available with these and other special features which make the policy more attractive:

Waiver of premium (Usually after a certain period of paid nursing home confinement, no additional premiums are required during the remainder of the covered confinement).

Home care benefit (Usually after a certain period of nursing home confinement, the policy will pay benefits when the patient returns home).

Automatic benefit increase (To offset the effects of inflation and future rising nursing home costs). A policy purchased today may not provide enough coverage if the patient enters a nursing home 10 or 15 years from now. For more meaningful protection, consider policies which automatically increase the daily benefit amount to help guard against rising nursing home costs in the future.

John and Shirley Hanson operate Hanson & Associates, The Woodlands, Texas.

How to Determine the Financial Strength of an Insurance Company

by George W. King

Today, more and more investors are taking advantage of the benefits offered by life insurance and annuities to help reach their long-term financial goals.

Safety, tax-deferred accumulation and income, guaranteed return on principal and interest are some of the benefits that make these products an attractive way to protect and increase the value of savings.

Because of today's economic conditions, it is important to know as much as possible about an insurance company before you invest your money. The following information will help you understand the factors used in evaluating a company's quality and financial strength.

Measuring Strength

Since insurance companies guarantee interest and invested principal in many of the products they issue, it is important for them to have a strong reputation for financial soundness and efficient asset management.

Each company is subject to the laws and regulations of the state in which it is licensed to do business, and is required to file a sworn statement of financial condition annually. In addition, each firm is reviewed and rated every year by A.M. Best Inc., which has been the recognized insurance rating agency for over 80 years.

A.M. Best reviews over 1,400 insurance firms and evaluates the various factors affecting the overall performance of a company to determine its relative financial strength and ability to meet contractual obligations. Only those insurers considered the most financially stable are awarded a superior (A+) or excellent (A) rating.

Key Financial Indicators

The A.M. Best rating focuses on several key factors:

Assets Under Management. Increasing assets are generally a good indication of a viable and growing organization.

Capital and Surplus. Increasing capital and surplus values generally mean that a company is operating profitably after meeting debt requirements and current expenses.

Profitability. A review of earnings' history indicates whether a company is operating at a profit.

Asset Reserves. Insurance companies are required to reserve assets to meet their liability for client obligations. An insurer's portfolio should be well diversified among stocks, bonds, cash and cash equivalents as well as among various companies and industries. Bonds in the portfolio should have varying maturities and higher than average quality.

Company History. The length of time a company has been in business, the effectiveness of its management and soundness of its strategic plans also contribute to overall strength.

In addition, we feel investors should be aware of several other factors:

1. There is a trade off between performance and peace of mind. If a company offers a higher interest rate than is currently available across the industry, you should expect higher risks, even though there is more opportunity for reward.
2. When dealing with A or A+ rated companies, the differences in the ratings are minor, so focusing on those differences would be a disservice to the companies.
3. Under state regulations, payment of the interest guaranteed in the contract must be met; however, in general, performance of the assets underlying the contract will fluctuate with market conditions and is not guaranteed.

George W. King is vice president of Advest, Inc., Lutherville, Maryland.

5

⬚⬚⬚⬚⬚⬚⬚⬚⬚⬚⬚⬚⬚⬚⬚⬚⬚⬚⬚⬚⬚⬚⬚

LIFESTYLE TOPICS

New Horizons in Retirement

by Alice and Fred Lee

"It's not your father's Oldsmobile!"—the punch line in GM's current TV ad campaign. Offspring of notables speak out about all the changes as they drive along in their new Olds. An effective ad.

A parallel—"It's not your father's retirement!" Today's retirees have a new world waiting for them. Completely different from their father's retirement. Not at all like the old traditional—buy a small place in Florida, fish from the city pier and then rock on the porch as the sun goes down!

For the past eight years, we have surveyed hundreds of retirement communities, villages and facilities in 31 states. We set out to see and experience the changes that have taken place and to find out what retirees do. On site, one-on-one discussions with hundreds of retirees, administrators, and counselors gave us answers to our research question. We identified 14 Lifestyle Options.

Four categories of change have heavily influenced the options that are available to today's retirees:

1. *Increased Life Expectancy.* The Bureau of Census Report (1985): White females at 60 can expect to live to 82.6; at 65 to 83.7; at 70 to 85. White males at age 60 to 78; at 65 to 79.6; and at 70 to 81.6. Blacks can expect to live 5 to 6½ years less than whites.

2. *Earlier Retirement.* The book "Age Wave", lists 60.2 as the average retirement age. Figures from Social Security indicate that since 1970, age 62 has replaced 65 and retirement increasingly occurs before 62.

3. *Women's Equality.* Changes in the laws, involvement and greater self-awareness have resulted in women refusing to conform to past gender roles. "It's not your mother's retirement" is applicable.

4. *Greater Financial Resources.* Many of today's retirees have a good nest egg. They have enjoyed career advances, pension and stock option plans, Social Security benefit increases, and in many cases, two incomes after the kids left home. Coupled with that, they had an ingrained need to save and prepare for the future.

From these changes there has been created a NEW WINDOW OF OPPORTUNITY. From age 60 to approximately 75, retirees can look forward to 15 years of involved activity. These are truly the Golden Years.

We call this Phase I of Retirement. During these years, health problems become an increasing concern, but most people can handle these as irritations.

Life continues on with few limitations if we maintain a positive attitude, that "can do" attitude our parents taught us during our developmental years which coincided with the depression and WWII.

Phase II covers the later years when aging and health problems take their toll.

Hundreds of discussions with those thinking about retirement highlighted another major problem. People don't know what to do, they don't know what Lifestyle Options are available.

The major thrust of pre-retirement planning assistance is financial planning. This is of prime importance. However, if the awareness of the need for financial planning takes place one to three years before scheduled retirement, it's probably too late.

We accept the importance of retirement income, but we conclude: financial planning provides security; lifestyle planning provides happiness.

Add a natural reluctance on the part of many not to want to think about aging and making retirement plans, and procrastination becomes the easy way out. Why?

We have been conditioned that when you retire, you're through. This carries with it a sense of uselessness, of being out of the mainstream, of being "old."

"Webster's New World Dictionary" definition of retirement is: To give up one's work, business career, etc. because of advanced age; retreat or withdraw to a secluded place; withdraw from use; apart from the world.

Add to the above: Social Security penalties for earning over a certain amount, many firms' Golden Handshake, the corporate emphasis on youth and it's easy to perceive you're old, we don't need you, here's a watch, goodbye.

In reality, this worthlessness is not true. The "New Window of Opportunity" offers years of exciting contribution, activity and personal fulfillment. The key to this attainment is self-responsibility.

At retirement no longer are there company imposed hours and schedules. A retiree picks up 2500+ new freedom hours in a year. How will these be utilized? Will it be finding ways to kill time or will each day be filled with exciting opportunities?

Lifestyle planning is vital. No one can do it for a retiree. Self-responsibility for action must be accepted even though it's a new experience. Most people are not used to making these personal decisions. They have been programmed by others all their lives,

now it's an individual responsibility. It's not an easy task.

14 Lifestyle Options

From our research, 14 distinct lifestyle options emerged. In our four-hour Lifestyle Seminar we discuss these options through a photographic slide trip around the country.

We wrote an 85,000 word manuscript on retirement lifestyles and our Literary Agent has concluded contract negotiations with a major publisher. Following is the summary description of each Lifestyle chapter in our book:

Phase I Lifestyle Choices

Stay put or move. Kids gone, house too big . . . Relocate . . . Where . . . New town . . . Plus and minus of moving . . . Effect on Lifestyle. LIFESTYLE OPTION #1—STAY PUT IN THE COMMUNITY.

Snowbirds/winter Texans. To the warm winter . . . Two houses . . . Buy . . . Rent . . . Pull your own . . . Geographic preferences . . . The extended vacation. LIFESTYLE OPTION #2—WINTER RESIDENT.

RV nomading—Full or part-time. What kind of rig . . . On the road, full or part time . . . Lifetime membership campgrounds . . . Boondocking . . . Alone or caravan . . . R.V. clubs . . . Full-time togetherness. LIFESTYLE OPTION #3—RV'ING.

Retirement Areas. What kind of climate—snowbelt—frostbelt—sunbelt . . . living predominantly with retirees or in any town U.S.A. LIFESTYLE OPTION #4—RETIREMENT AREA LIVING.

Club/resort/vacation community. Where . . . Hills . . . Pine lands . . . Desert . . . Along the beach . . . Big . . . Little . . . Temperate climate . . . Tropical Climate. LIFESTYLE OPTION #5—LEISURE/SOCIAL CENTERED LIVING.

Large Retirement Village/City. Self-contained environment . . . Homes—all sizes . . . Social . . . Sports . . . Clubs . . . Churches . . . Synagogue . . . Shopping . . . Medical Center . . . Police/Fire protection . . . Community pride . . . Resident's Association . . . Retirees all the time. LIFESTYLE OPTION #6—RETIREE DOMINATED LIVING.

Total Planned Community. Segregated areas—Retirees—Families with children—Families without children—Singles—Commercial . . . Self-contained . . . Strong community involvement. LIFESTYLE OPTION #7—PLANNED INTERGENERATIONAL LIVING.

Small retirement community. Clear cut restricted neighborhood in a city . . . Majority retirees . . . Centralized meeting/activity center . . . Planned socials . . . Community loyalty/pride . . . Much belonging . . . Neighborliness . . . Activities outside the neighborhood. LIFESTYLE OPTION #8—PARTIAL RETIREE DOMINATED LIVING.

Pau Hana in Hawaii. Which island . . . Big city—Honolulu . . . Small town true Hawaii . . . Winter resident or full time . . . Four-tier cultural pecking order . . . Living in another culture . . . Searching/finding/living the true Hawaiian spirit. LIFESTYLE OPTION #9—HAWAIIAN LIVING.

Foreign Retirement. Major change . . . Where . . . For how long . . . Considerable flexibility a must . . . Personal attitude about foreigners . . . Acceptance difference living standards, ways, views, values . . . Need for thorough research, lengthy try out. LIFESTYLE OPTION #10—FOREIGN LIVING.

Special Interest. Retirement community: On a college campus—at a religious retreat facility—adjacent to military bases—as part of a nudist colony . . . houseboating . . . education, formal degrees or Elderhostel . . . kid following. LIFESTYLE OPTION #11—SPECIAL INTEREST.

Entering phase II of retirement. Preparing for the inevitable slowdown. Considerations have to include—what if I/we live to be 80 or possibly 90+? Will we remain independent or be a burden on the kids?

Phase II Lifestyle Choices

Retirement Residence. Deluxe apartment/dormitory . . . All seniors . . . Services . . . Meals . . . Few responsibilities . . . Commonality of interests . . . Active living . . . Not many worries . . . Complete freedom. LIFESTYLE OPTION #12—PHASE TWO CAREFREE LIVING.

Retirement complex—available health care. Deluxe apartment . . . cottage . . . All Services . . . Carefree active living . . . On site 24-hour emergency medical and health care—Pay as you use basis . . . Comfort knowing help is available when needed . . . Good secure feeling. LIFESTYLE OPTION #13—PHASE TWO CARE WHEN NEEDED.

Continuing care/life care community (CC/LCC). Deluxe apartment . . . cottage . . . All services . . . Living a full life . . . contractual guarantee for life—housing—services—all medical care . . . Cocoonlike lifetime security. LIFESTYLE OPTION #14—PHASE TWO CARE FOR LIFE SECURITY.

One other major problem must be addressed. How do you get people to take action? To accept the inevitability of retirement and when a spouse is concerned to start open dialogue about "what we will do in retirement."

Too many people let retirement happen—reactive rather than proactive. In our seminars we provide forms which require individual evaluation of each lifestyle. The two lists are then combined. This forces open dialogue in order to come up with a plan.

The same process is applied to the determination of individual activities as the question of 2500+ new-found hours is addressed. If a lifestyle decision can't be reached, the question—Do you want to retire or continue working?—then becomes paramount. If we can influence people to take a proactive approach to retirement lifestyles, our mission will have been accomplished.

Phase Two—The Later Years of Retirement

Stay in your own home as long as you can! Everyone has heard this advice. It's always been touted as the way to live out your later years. We don't agree. We feel there are some very good alternatives that should be considered.

In fact, we have made up our minds not to spend our later years in our present home. In our mid '50s we down-sized from a large home to a patio home. Even though it's all on one floor, brick, no steps, no lawn, and has a sprinkler system, we will eventually move. We don't know exactly where or when, but we've decided we will move to a retirement community with adjacent health care.

Strong words! Very opinionated! True. Here's why.

Let's go back to the title of this section—specifically, Phase Two—the Later Years of Retirement. What does that mean? You're no different on day one of retirement than you were the day before. But as retirement progresses, illness, disease or just normal aging, will cause changes in your lifestyle. You will slow down. Not stop. Just do fewer things and at a slightly slower pace. That's when Phase Two of retirement comes into being.

No one can tell when Phase Two will commence. There is no specific age when you find yourself crossing the line. Each person is different. Accordingly, normal aging and health problems vary with each individual. When it arrives, there is an increasing need for assistance, which will be in direct proportion to the degree of physical decline that takes place. The decline may be abrupt or progress very slowly over a period of many years.

We feel there are two options:

1. The Traditional—Remain in the homestead.

As long as there is sufficient self-mobility and mental keenness, this is workable. If one is lucky enough to have a cadre of friendly old-time neighbors who are assistance-minded, the occasional call for a helping hand will be answered. A person's church group may also provide the occasional helping hand.

When the need progresses from occasional to frequent, the assistance giver may well become busy with other things. Plus, the old-time neighbors have their own problems, including their need for assistance.

Death takes its toll. New neighbors will not feel the same allegiance as the old neighbors. Our mobile society is not conducive to old-time neighborliness.

As the neighborhood changes, hopefully it upgrades, but if it downgrades, the element of personal safety becomes a new concern. As you read in the papers, the incidence of mugging of the elderly is high. Not just in the rough areas of town, it's widespread in all areas.

What about the children as caregivers? If one is fortunate enough to have "the kids" in the same town, assistance could be forthcoming. As needs progress, the assistance demands will become quite a burden. These are some logical questions. (1) Do you want to be dependent on your kids? Do you want to burden them with making decisions for you? (2) What is fair to expect from the kids?

While waiting in the doctor's office for a flu shot, Fred observed first hand a "need" case. A lady wearing an emergency call button around her neck was paying her bill. She asked the receptionist to write out in big letters on a full sheet of paper the instructions on the prescription. She had broken her glasses a while back and couldn't see to read. In order to pay the fee for her call, she also asked for help in filling out the check, which she would then sign.

Another request was to tell her where to sign the Medicare form. She asked if anyone knew the whereabouts of a mailbox. A gentleman said "about two blocks down the street." Unfortunately her reply was that she couldn't walk that far. The clerk said she would mail it for her.

Alice has seen many, many pathetic cases of the elderly trying to manage at home. She has distributed meals as part of the Meals on Wheels program. Some homesteads are run down and the inside a cluttered mess—many of these are homes in what could be considered a nice part of town.

There is a great personal reward in chatting with these folks, but it's hard to break away. They need so desperately the smile and companionship of anyone—even a stranger who brings them a hot meal.

All around us are the invisible elderly!

The lady in the doctor's office, the recipients of Meals on Wheels are fighters. That's good. But the odds are stacked against them. There is another option where the odds are much better.

2. Move to a retirement community.

An immediate point of clarification. Our retirement lifestyle research has taken us throughout the country since 1982. We have found many facilities that use the word "retirement" in their title when in reality they are convalescent or nursing homes. This is not what we mean when we use the term retirement community. In fact, to become a part of a retirement community

you must be completely self-sufficient in all respects!

We will not impose our needs on friends or family and force difficult decisions on our two sons. While we are still able to handle our affairs, we will move to a retirement community with adjacent health care facilities. When we need help it will be readily available, in surroundings familiar to us, staffed by professionals we know, and easily accessible to our support group—our friends in the retirement community.

For us, the key element is a desire to make our own decisions (not burden the children) and ultimately enjoy a greater degree of happiness.

For example, we've observed those who chose to remain in their own home beyond the point of being able to enter a retirement community. When a serious health problem did occur, it was necessary to go to a nursing home or some other facility for assisted living.

Many times this was in a new community, usually near one of the children. Unfortunately, there were no old friends or familiar support groups. On the other hand, if a person chooses to enter a retirement community before a severe health problem occurs, there are many advantages. They can become involved in the local community surrounding the retirement facility, a church, social clubs, etc., in accordance with personal choice.

We feel this is the way to go! What are your plans for Phase Two—the later years of retirement?

The Lees reside in Richardson, Texas.

Geographically . . . Where People Choose to Spend Their Retirement Years Can Have a Significant Impact on Retirement Success

by L. Malcolm Rodman

Most retirees, demographers tell us, choose to stay in their home communities, close to family and life-long friends, as well as familiar surroundings and services.

Others migrate, to get away from cold climates and big city bustle, to enjoy new friendships, new leisure and the warmer climate of the Sunbelt states. A still smaller percentage chooses to live overseas, either to return to ancestral societies or to live like royalty on Social Security.

Approaching retirement for most present-day Americans offers options and possibilities of where to live undreamed of by their grandparents. Two generations back, the "granny shack" at the rear of the family homestead, or mother's room upstairs, was not uncommon.

Gone forever are the days when several generations of a family could claim a single community as "home". Instead, today's retiree is apt to spend a considerable amount of time jetting or driving around the country, to keep up with children and grandchildren.

To say that pre-retirees have a world of choice is no exaggeration.

Statistics show that most retirees stay in their hometown; and a significant percentage of those who move away, eventually return. This suggests that any relocation option must be weighed carefully against the pros and cons of staying put. One might choose to remain in his or her home community, but to trade-down to a smaller house, apartment or condo; or buy into a life care or retirement community.

Approaching Relocation Options

Now, to those relocation options. There are two basic approaches one might employ as suggested by the five books listed at the end of this article.

Author Peter Dickinson uses the methodology of hitting the road as a traveler, to see and learn for one's self. Each of his books on retirement edens—in the Sunbelt; in the other 37 United States; and abroad—are based upon his personal observations, gathered during years of travel. His impressions are supplemented by interviews with retirees, AARP groups, plus data supplied by local Aging agencies.

In the "Places Rated" books, all the communities are compared and rated according to a set of factors. These include factors such as costs of living, housing, health care, safety, cultural and recreation opportunities. The communities are then arrayed, in descending order, by individual factor; then by their cumulative scores.

This is an attempt to apply some rational standards to what has to be a highly individualized judgment. The books point out that all factors do not have equal weight for everyone; and each volume poses a series of questions to help the reader

Census statistics show that 47 out of 50 older adults stay at their present address. One in 29 of them stays in the same town, but moves to smaller quarters.

Only one in every 73 of them moves to another part of the state, perhaps to occupy a former vacation home full time. Only about one in every 94 older adults moves to another state.

Even these figures do not tell the full story. Studies of older adults who move to another state show a surprising number of them either returned home or moved to still another state within a decade.

At a minimum, these statistics should compel pre-retirees to weigh the options very carefully before deciding to pull up stakes and relocate to another part of the country.

Sun Belt Keeps Growing

Looking at another set of statistics, America's southwestern states, plus Florida, will lead the nation in population and economic growth through the end of the century, according to the Commerce Department.

Nevada and Arizona will show the fastest growth rates in personal income, jobs and population. One out of every six jobs created in this decade will be in California. Also, Utah and Hawaii are predicted to grow rapidly, along with Florida. Texas is expected to continue its recovery from the oil price drop of the 1980s, adding one million new jobs and seeing personal income rise dramatically.

The migration of older adults to the Sun Belt continues to be a contributing factor to the population growth of these states.

Shift to Rural Counties

Another demographic trend is attributed primarily to retirees—the shift away from America's large cities to rural areas in all parts of the nation. According to the Department of Agriculture, there are about 500 rural counties in the nation being "gentrified" by an inflow of retirees seeking to escape big city congestion, crime and pollution.

Such counties range from Pennsylvania's Pocono Mountains to Michigan's Upper Peninsula, and include California's Gold Rush country and East Texas' Piney Woods.

Confirming other statistics showing many retirees staying in their home states, these counties are often on the fringe of metropolitan suburbs, in places known to retirees, where many already have second homes.

During the 1980s, these counties experienced a growth rate triple the average for all rural counties, and nearly double the growth in urban areas.

8 States Host Half of All Retirees

Approximately half of the nation's 28 million retirees, aged 65 or older, lived in just eight states in 1987: California, New York and Florida had about two million each; and Pennsylvania, Ohio, Illinois, Michigan and Texas had more than a million each. Florida has the highest percentage of over 65 residents—17.6 percent.

Over 65 Population Ballooning

Trends cited above will accelerate as older Americans stay healthier longer and live longer.

In the 1980 census, there were more than 5.3 million people age 65 years or older in the U.S. The government expects the 1990 census to show more than 31 million, and by the year 2000, it projects 34 million Americans over age 65.

construct a personal scale of most important factors.

This might prompt an individual to
choose a locale with a warm climate, low state
taxes, small town tranquillity, with low housing and living costs which would let one get
by on little more than a Social Security check.

Others might opt for a location with a
harsher climate, higher state taxes, and higher
living costs in exchange for the recreation,
sports and cultural offerings of a university
town or a major metropolitan area.

Dickinson's Approach

As companion books, *Sunbelt Retirement*
and *Retirement Edens Outside the Sunbelt*
represent travel guides offering pre-retirees
an introduction to each state including a
discussion of climate, living costs, availability
of health care and recreational opportunities.

For most states, the author offers his
personal ratings of retirement areas as excellent, good, adequate and poor.

He is generous with names and addresses
of agencies for obtaining more information
on localities, including chambers of commerce, realtors' groups, medical and hospital associations, and aging agencies.

In *Sunbelt Retirement,* the author offers
a checklist for sizing up any community
covering the following categories: climate
and environmental factors—pollution, noise,
health aspects and medical facilities, housing
costs and availability, cost of living, leisure-
time activities and special services and
facilities for seniors.

In his second book, he lists his criteria
for identifying a retirement "Eden":

1. Climate—the most days with a
   temperature of 66 degrees F and
   humidity 55 percent.
2. Cost of living—where a retired couple
   can live for around $13,000 annually,
   and pay eight percent or less in state
   and local taxes.
3. Housing—obtain a two-bedroom home
   from $50,000.
4. Medical facilities—semiprivate
   hospital rooms for less than $250
   daily, and at least one doctor per
   750 residents.
5. Recreation and culture—a place where
   someone interested in books, music
   or art would feel comfortable.
6. Special services for seniors—including
   transportation and facilities.

Keep in mind this book was updated in
1987, so costs and prices in these projections will be understated, due to inflation.

While many of the famous retirement
communities in Florida and Arizona receive
extensive coverage, the author points pre-
retirees to other areas as well. Among his
choices for excellent sunbelt "havens": Chapel
Hill, Henderson, Tryon and Brevard,
NC; St. Simons Island and Jekyll Island,
GA; Covington and Abita Springs, LA;
Mountain Home and Eureka Springs, AR;
Roswell, NM.

Outside the sunbelt states, he gives excel-
lent ratings to communities such as: Camden,
ME; Hanover and Nashua, NH; Lichtfield,
CT; Cooperstown, NY; Carlisle, PA; Easton
and Salisbury, MD; Charlottesville and
Lynchburg, VA; Princeton, IL; Green Bay,
WI; Boulder and Durango, CO; Cedar City
and St. George, UT; Monterey, Sonoma and
Nevada City, CA; Eugene and Ashland, OR;
and Seattle and Sequim, WA.

Hawaii, a paradise in most respects, is
red-flagged because of the highest housing
and living costs in the nation; plus the high
costs of air trips back to the mainland to
keep in touch with family.

These volumes reinforce the dictum—
there's no one perfect place for everyone. If
there was, it sure would be crowded!

They also reinforce the advice given by retirement planners that pre-retirees "rehearse" for retirement, by making repeated and extended visits to any new part of the country they have in mind as a retirement haven. There is no substitute for living there, meeting the people and deciding if the place is "right" for you. This is especially important before selling a home and relocating.

Retirement Housing Options

In both books, Dickinson describes various retirement communities in the states he discusses. Such housing/health care arrangements are worthy of consideration by "older" adults, say those age 75 and older.

When these communities were first developed some years ago by various church denominations, they received negative publicity due to a few scattered abuses.

At the outset, many of them required their clientele to sign over most of their assets in exchange for a lifetime guarantee of shelter and health care. Some church groups were unable to manage investments wisely, and became unable to meet their commitments.

Such early problems have been overcome, by and large, by non-profit sponsors. A new generation of proprietary developer has appeared on the scene as well.

The field has matured with the advent of repurchase guarantees, less expensive admission fees, and outright rental or lease offerings.

Major hotel chains, like Hyatt and Marriott, have entered the field to put to work their expertise in real estate development, lodging and food management.

In the conventional housing field, home builders are designing and building smaller homes containing amenities and safety features which appeal to an older clientele.

The timing and sale of one's long-time residence, along with the purchase of a new property, requires planning preferably with the advice of an accountant or tax specialist.

Many pre-retirees live in housing which has appreciated far beyond their original investment plus the one-time $125,000 tax exclusion (if they qualify for this). This means a healthy income tax bite from the proceeds of the sale of a residence unless the seller is prepared to re-invest in another residence within a relatively short period of time.

Thus, pre-retirees, whether they plan to remain in their hometowns or relocate, have a wide and growing choice of housing options. Some of these options will have tax implications as well.

The "Places Rated" Methodology

According to *Retirement Places Rated*, America's top five retirement localities are:

1. Murray-Kentucky Lake, KY

2. Clayton-Clarkesville, GA

3. Hot Springs-Lake Ouachita, AR

4. Grand Lake-Lake Tenkiller, OK

5. Fayetteville, AR

According to *Places Rates Almanac*, America's top five "best places to live" metropolitan areas, for persons of any age, are:

1. Seattle, WA

2. San Francisco, CA

3. Pittsburgh, PA

4. Washington, DC-MD-VA

5. San Diego, CA

The lists do not coincide because the surveys were done at different times, using different criteria, and comparing different groupings of communities. Indeed, only San Diego, from the second list, was even compared in the first grouping.

Retirement Places Rated compared 131 communities in 38 states that, in the opinion of the authors, reflect the preferences of many mobile retired persons. Thus many areas, especially large metropolitan areas, were omitted.

Places Rated Almanac, a more ambitious effort, ranks all 333 U.S. metropolitan areas; being cities of at least 50,000 population, or an urbanized area of at least 50,000 located in a county or counties with a total population of at least 100,000.

Each book compares and rates each community according to a number of factors— living costs, job outlook, crime, health, transportation, education, the arts, recreation and climate. Since the *Places Rated Almanac* is meant to be a guide for younger families, concerned with jobs and schooling for children, it includes factors not especially vital to retirees.

Retirement Places Rated is more specific to retirees' interests. For example, it discusses the availability of part time employment in each community on the premise that many retirees will need or want to work part time.

Cost of Living Important

It puts heavy emphasis on the costs of living in retirement, especially on states with the highest and lowest local income, sales and property taxes.

For retirees with limited means, the tax picture can be important.

For a typical year, 1986, when the U.S. average per capita tax burden of state and local taxes was $805, it was only $390 in

Montana and $462 in Mississippi. At the other end of the scale, it was $1,073 in Massachusetts, $1,163 in Hawaii and $1,266 in New York.

In recent years, most states have imposed new taxes—so taxes are rising everywhere, more than offsetting Federal tax reductions— and retirement planners should caution their clientele that yesterday's low tax state may not necessarily remain so. It will pay to get updated information.

Both housing and monthly living expenses can vary widely; being most expensive in large metropolitan areas.

The "Places Rated" volumes rate warmer climates as the most desirable for retirement. Of the 20 top rated communities for climate, *Retirement Places Rated* has 15 of them in Florida.

Health care gets full attention in both volumes, including the number and quality of hospital beds and the number of physicians per capita.

Living costs, health care and climate are not the sole factors pre-retirees must consider. The value in these books, used as workbooks, are in the number and variety of other considerations it encourages one to make before deciding upon relocation.

What recreational facilities are available? Are there good restaurants? A theater group? Is the community served by a public TV station? Is the crime rate at an acceptable level? Is there adequate public transportation? What are the opportunities for continuing education?

The Top Choices

To give you an idea of how the methodology works, the authors explain why Murray-Kentucky Lake, KY finishes first in the list of 131 retirement places rated.

This is an area composed of Calloway and Marshall counties in Western Kentucky.

It rates so high because of low health care and housing costs, excellent access to accredited hospitals, a high rating for personal safety, a good supply of physicians and medical specialists, an established public transit system, opportunity for continuing education at a mid-size state university and a huge body of inland water along its eastern border.

In the *Places Rated Almanac,* Seattle rates as the nation's most livable town, compared with 332 other metropolitan areas. It ranked first in recreational opportunities, and high for health care and the environment, transportation facilities, the arts and climate. It has a good job market. Yet, it places first despite being one of the nation's more expensive places to live, with a relatively high crime rate.

Even the "best" places aren't perfect!

Whatever community a pre-retiree might be considering, the factors described in these books provide a factual framework for determining the good and bad points of a potential retirement town.

Thus, they can reinforce a pre-retiree's instincts that a place "feels right"; or may give one pause for further consideration.

Bias against the Big Cities

Taken as a group, the five resource books cited seem to indicate that those retirees who do relocate will opt for the smaller cities in the sunbelt states.

There may be a significant exception to this rule: the well-off retirees from executive ranks, who may opt for the big city excitement, the cultural and artistic offerings, the major league sports and the other attractions of America's major cities.

These areas score high in the *Places Rated Almanac* because of their leisure time and cultural offerings, which have a high appeal to a segment of the retiree community. To enjoy these offerings, these retirees may be willing to accept, and can afford, higher taxes and costs of living. As for harsh climates—there's always the extended winter vacation trip.

So, again, the retirement planner will be advised not to jump to conclusions; or to accept someone else's idea of a retirement haven as the perfect choice for his or her clientele.

Retiring Overseas

Living overseas is an idea which appeals to a limited number of retirees. Peter A. Dickinson notes in *Travel and Retirement Edens Abroad* that each month the Social Security Administration sends about 330,000 checks overseas to retired workers and their dependents. (While Social Security benefits will follow a retiree overseas, Medicare benefits do not).

It is not necessary to give up one's U.S. citizenship and purchase property overseas to enjoy living abroad. Many more retirees choose extended vacations abroad, say from three to six months, in rental properties found in many places—Mexico, the Caribbean, the Mediterranean coasts of Spain or Portugal, Yugoslavia, Cost Rica.

One of the main attractions of these overseas destinations is the low living costs, which permit retirees to live better than at home on modest pensions.

For another group of retirees, overseas living means returning to the "old country" of their birth, to live out their remaining years with family.

Dickinson devotes the bulk of his book to those locales where substantial numbers of Americans have retired—the islands of the Caribbean, Mexico, Costa Rica and Canada.

More sketchy is his review of retirement in Europe, Israel, Australia and Asia. As with possible retirement havens within the U.S., the search for overseas locales might be the subject of a number of trips by pre-retirees.

Having It Both Ways

As noted earlier, retirement relocation need not be an either-or proposition: stay put or relocate. The books noted above can be useful for pre-retirees searching out new vacation destinations, or places they might want to spend part of the year.

Several million retirees are roaming the country in recreation vehicles, either full time or part of the year.

Conclusion: A Challenge for Planners

Some areas of retirement planning lend themselves to a very disciplined curriculum: the nature of a firm's pension benefits; Social Security benefits for workers and dependents; purchasing health insurance to supplement Medicare.

Not so when it comes to retirement relocation decisions. Here the choices are multiple and the impact upon a successful retirement vary substantially. There is no set formula which most can follow.

Instead, these are highly individualized decisions, which can be made only by the retiree and his or her spouse. The retirement planner can help the clientele understand the complexity of the situation, and teach how to obtain facts and weigh them carefully, before making decisions.

Teaching the clientele how to make informed decisions in this area is the greatest service a retirement planner can provide.

The following books were reviewed in this article. Note that each is updated from time to time; so be sure to ask for the most current edition.

Books by Peter A. Dickinson, published by AARP Books, 1900 Lake Avenue, Glenview, Ill. 60025:

Sunbelt Retirement. The complete state-by-state guide to retiring in the South and West of the United States.

Retirement Edens Outside the Sunbelt. A complete guide to the best places for retirees in 37 states.

Travel and Retirement Edens Abroad. Identifies retirement edens in Mexico, Canada, Costa Rica, the Caribbean, Europe, Israel, Australia and the Far East.

Books by Richard Boyer and David Savageau:

Places Rated Almanac. Prentice Hall Travel, 15 Columbus Circle, New York, N.Y. 10023. Guide to finding the best places to live in America; ranks and compares all 333 metropolitan areas for living costs, job outlook, crime, health, transportation, education, the arts, recreation and climate.

Retirement Places Rated. Prentice Hall Travel, 15 Columbus Circle, New York, N.Y. 10023. Ranks 131 retirement locales in the U.S. on climate, money matters, housing, health care, services, personal safety and recreation.

Mr. Rodman is Executive Director of ISRP.

Reports of Couples in the First Year of Retirement: Pleasures and Peeves

by Barbara H. Vinick, Ph.D. and David J. Ekerdt, Ph.D.

This article will present perceptions of married couples in the first year of retirement—a stage of life which evokes contradictory images: In one, a couple is walking hand-in-hand on the beach as the tropical sun sets; in another, a husband in his undershirt lounges in an easy chair, beer in hand, as his wife attempts to mop under his feet.

We undertook the research on couples in retirement because, although there is today a general recognition that retirement is a family affair, affecting the spouse at least as much as the retiree, comparatively little is known about the transition which most married couples have come to expect.

The topic of marriage in retirement is an under-researched one. Most research still treats retirement as an individual phenomenon—understandable when so much of it is based on large national data sets with an emphasis on economic analysis.

As the population ages, the number of married retirees increases each year. The average age of retirement nationally (and in the sample of people we interviewed) is 62, so most people can look forward to a number of years in retirement with a spouse. Research which addresses their concerns becomes increasingly relevant.

The Study

In this research, we looked at the transition to retirement—the first year of retirement— among male retirees and their wives. We realize that women's retirement and family issues have received even less attention than men's. As women join the workforce in ever-increasing numbers, such research will become even more important.

However, we are affiliated with the Normative Aging Study, a bio-medical study of the normal aging process among men (Ekerdt, 1987). Our pool of potential respondents came from our contact with the 1,900 men who have participated in this study for twenty to twenty-five years. We therefore recruited couples according to the male partner's retirement, which we tracked by means of periodic postcard surveys. We did not ignore the wife's work history and retirement, data we collected and will continue to analyze, but our method of recruitment encouraged the focus on the effect of husbands' retirement on marriage.

We interviewed 92 couples in which the husband had been retired six to twelve months. Normative Aging Study participants reflect the demographic composition of the Boston area. They live in urban, suburban and some rural communities, generally within 50 miles of Boston. Not all are veterans, but they were free of chronic disease when screened initially, and had a commitment to staying in the area. To a great extent, they represent the core of stable, white, middle-class society, minus the extremes.

A few statistics about our study sample: The average age of the men we interviewed was 62 and the average age of wives was 60. One third of wives were working, half of those full-time, and half part-time. As for the husbands, 36% were working part-time, and the rest were not employed. Sixty percent of the men had been white-collar workers before retirement, and 40% had been blue-collar. Number of years married ranged from 15 to 46, with a mean of 36. Every couple had children, with an average of three, and 48% had at least one child living in the home (a somewhat surprisingly large proportion of stay-at-home or returning children, generally in their twenties.)

The majority of respondents were in good health according to self-evaluation. On a four-point scale from poor to excellent, no one rated health as poor, and 88% of men and 83% of women rated health as good or excellent. Respondents likewise saw themselves in good financial health. Over 90% of men and women agreed with the statements "We have enough (money) to get along, and even a little extra" or "we can buy pretty much anything we want with the income we now have."

Couples were interviewed simultaneously, but separately. We would not accept one spouse if the other refused. (When couples declined to participate, it was due to refusal on the part of wives, who had never previously been asked to take part in Normative Aging Study projects. This is unusual in couples research; men are generally the reluctant partners.)

The 90 minute face-to-face interview, which mixed open-ended queries and conversation with forced-choice items, was designed to disclose a broad picture of the transition from work to retirement—descriptions and evaluations by average couples, with special emphasis on the marital relationship.

We found that two items in the interview were particularly telling in summarizing husbands' and wives' responses to retirement. Near the end, after discussion of a wide variety of aspects of marriage and retirement, we asked them to recount the "best thing" about their/their husband's retirement and the "most difficult problem or hardest thing to get used to." This paper will report their responses—the results of coding, categorization and corroboration among three reviewers.

Results

Positive Aspects of Retirement

When men were asked to recount the best thing about retirement, almost everyone responded in terms of the same aspect. A whopping 89% praised the freedom to leave behind the pressures and the general tyranny of working life.

Time and again we heard the virtues of autonomy praised by those who now felt in control of daily routines for the first time in their adult lives. We had been unaware of the chains of captivity that work represented to so many of our male respondents, even those who were in positions of authority and who professed satisfaction with their work.

Although many mentioned their newfound ability to pursue interests and carry out projects which had previously been squeezed into limited time, the major emphasis was on leaving behind the rigid and dehumanizing requirements of working life— meeting others' expectations rather than one's own, the necessity of getting out in the morning at 6 AM in a blizzard, contending with the declining work ethic among younger co-workers or subordinates, difficulties of commuting to work, conflicts with bosses and colleagues, the constant pressure of deadlines.

They contrasted aspects such as those with current freedom to arrange daily activities according to their own desires—to get up in the morning when they pleased, to accomplish projects at their own pace, to determine leisure activities on the spur of the moment, to sit down and relax when they felt like it.

During the course of the interview, it was not uncommon for men to express pleasure concerning the increased amount of time they now had to spend with their wives. The majority enjoyed travel, day trips to visit relatives or friends, sports such as skiing or golf, dining out as a couple, or just companionably staying at home reading or watching television. However, only 11% reported marital companionship as the best aspect of retirement.

In contrast 39% of women reported that the best thing about husbands' retirement was the increased amount of time that it afforded to be together. Proximity encouraged feelings of greater marital closeness and companionship. Wives were getting to know husbands better as they shared leisure activities and the routines of daily life.

We had the impression that some wives had been fettered to a routine of housekeeping chores which had isolated them from the mainstream of the outside world, much as husbands had been shackled by work responsibilities. Now, as husbands were freed, those wives who were amenable also felt a new freedom from largely self-imposed daily isolation and humdrum routine.

Fully half of the wives reported that they appreciated the decrease in stress that retirement represented. Many said simply that they were happy because husbands were happy. Others, perhaps more reflective, recognized a more relaxed atmosphere in the home now that husbands were retired. Some observers have noted the "contagion"

of stress and depression from one person to another (Albrecht and Adelman, 1984).

It was as if women had caught the contagion of relaxation. They themselves felt more at ease now that husbands were calmer. Interactions were more satisfying, as several noted, now that husbands were more focused on what they were communicating rather than thinking about problems of the job. Husbands were less curt and less quick to anger—more patient and serene.

From these responses, difference according to gender becomes obvious: Men were "self-focused" and women were "spouse-focused." Men almost always responded in terms of individual criteria—achievement of a desired and prized quality of life relative to the status quo before retirement.

Women, on the other hand, almost always responded in terms of marital life—increased companionship, husbands' happier dispositions, and a more relaxed atmosphere in the home. Such gender differences may be due to the phrasing of questions in terms of "your retirement" and "your husband's retirement". It is more likely, however, that they reflect true differences in men's and women's orientations.

Women's socialization and life experiences generally have enabled them to "specialize" in creating and maintaining personal relationships. In the absence of the intimate relationships with friends and other family members that women have typically forged, men rely heavily on marriage for satisfaction of social needs (Blau, 1973). But the "instrumental" bias encourages evaluation of satisfaction in terms of personal criteria, rather than the affiliative criteria of wives.

Negative Aspects of Retirement

The same gender difference in focus was exhibited when we asked husbands and wives to describe any difficulties, problems, or the hardest thing to get used to in regard to retirement.

Of the 68% of men who recognized that some area had necessitated adjustment when they retired (32% insisted that nothing at all had been difficult or hard to get used to), all but a handful indicated issues at the individual level. A quarter of the men noted some difficulty in adjusting to lack of structure that work had formerly imposed upon their daily routines.

Many did not know what to do with themselves, citing too much idle time. They sometimes felt bored and uninterested, especially in winter, when bad weather forced them to stay indoors. Many had not developed interests earlier in life, when they could pursue as retirees; others were devotees of activities that could be enjoyed only in temperate weather, such as gardening and golf. We noticed that variations in Boston weather influenced activities considerably, often resulting in different evaluations of time use in retirement depending on the season. We interviewed more men suffering from ennui in February than in June.

In contrast to the majority of men in this group, a few claimed that the problem with time use derived from having too much to do. They berated themselves for not being able to set priorities, in some cases not accomplishing household maintenance and renovation tasks that they had included in pre-retirement agendas. While most men reveled in the sense of relaxation and leisure that retirement engendered ("If I don't do it today, I'll do it tomorrow"), those few were particularly hard on themselves, as they spoke of falling behind self-imposed schedules.

Twenty-three percent of the male respondents stated that they missed some aspect of their former work—the most prevalent being interaction with former co-workers. Many men in the sample had little or no contact with friends, besides social engagements as a couple with other couples. They missed the daily give and take entailed in working with others. Some kept in touch by regular visits to the workplace, but most felt that such sojourns were inappropriate and even unwanted.

Others missed the sense of responsibility, prestige or power that work provided. They were aware of a decrease in status that accompanied the transition from work to retirement. Although they professed to be satisfied in retirement, some men felt a certain amount of guilt, and a few even projected those feelings onto others, claiming that neighbors and relatives wondered why they had retired instead of continuing to earn an honest living.

Ten percent mentioned financial concerns—worry over whether they would have enough money in the future to maintain present lifestyles, difficulties making ends meet, or decisions concerning income. A mere 8% noted the marital relationship as the most difficult aspect of retirement. Those few alluded to conflict and lack of communication.

Contrary to husbands, of those wives who reported some difficulty (20% could think of nothing to which they had to adjust), responses almost always referred to issues of relationship with the spouse. Fifty-seven percent cited problems of what we have called "impingement"—overlap of the husband into the wife's sphere of activity, as he spent more time in the home.

Housewives mentioned disruption of home maintenance schedules they had developed over the years or not getting as much done around the house. Some were distressed by husbands' criticism of their efficiency in housekeeping or their suggestions. When housekeeping standards of partners were not the same, some wives were discomforted by messy hobbies, reading materials left lying around and use of the dining room table for part-time jobs. Working women cited delay in getting out of the house in the morning, as relaxed husbands wanted conversation. Others felt a certain amount of envy as husbands were able to remain in bed as they scurried about.

Many wives cited a lack of privacy. What had previously been an exclusive household realm was now open to scrutiny. Husbands could overhear telephone conversations. They could monitor wives' daily routines. They were just there. Furthermore, it was common for wives to feel uneasy about leaving husbands at home if they went out. Wives reported that initially they felt a kind of guilt, even though it was rare for husbands to express disappointment or demand companionship.

Another ten percent of women noted some characteristic of the spouse with which they had difficulty—ill health, depression, lack of activity, annoying behavior, failure to communicate. A few mentioned financial uncertainties (5%), and coping with moving (4%).

Discussion and Implications

As indicated previously, comparison of men's and women's responses suggests that spouse-focused issues are particularly salient among women, as are self-focused issues among men in the first year of retirement. Further comparison within genders suggests that ambivalence is a feature of the first year of retirement—certainly at the group level and often at the individual level, as respondents noted satisfactions and difficulties concerning the same aspects of retirement.

Thus, men said that freedom from external control and job pressures were the best things about retirement; but, at the same time, they also struggled to adjust to that very lack of external control and structure

that the job provided and to find substitutions for the positive self-feelings that the job generated. Similarly, wives were pleased with the increased amount of time with spouses, which formed that basis for closer and more vital relationships.

At the same time, they were concerned with intrusion by husbands into formerly private domains, caused by that same increase in togetherness.

It is important to state that overall the gains outweighed the drawbacks for the majority of respondents. Global evaluations of retirement were generally positive: For example, when asked to place themselves on a nine-rung ladder from "extremely unhappy" (with retirement) at the bottom to "extremely happy" at the top, 66% of husbands and 65% or wives placed themselves on the top two rungs. Sixty percent of men and women described the quality of life as "somewhat" or "much" better since the husband's retirement, and less than 10% described it as worse.

Analysis of case studies written after each interview supports a positive picture of retirement. For most people, the transition had been comparatively easy. Some were still coming to grips with the change, but others, including most of the women who talked about issues of impingement, said that difficulties had been short lived—a period of weeks or months—or that they had been minor to begin with. Neither our results nor the research findings of other studies suggest that retirement should be considered a crisis in the lives of married couples.

Results suggest some implications for advising couples prior to retirement. Because retirement represents a passage from one state of life to another, with accompanying role changes, most people will feel the necessity to adjust to some aspect of the transition—missing work, idle time, lack of privacy, change in routine. A few respondents claimed that life was just the same, but perhaps denial of change was a way of coping. Recent retirees should not be surprised if there is a period of uncertainty, of feeling positive and dubious at the same time. Such ambivalence may be a normal part of adjustment, and, generally, positive sentiments will predominate.

Few people claimed that the transition had been very difficult, and the majority of husbands and wives were satisfied with life in retirement six to twelve months after the event. When couples were unhappy, it was mainly due to circumstances external to retirement itself (such as ill health of one of the partners or problems of other family members) or a history of marital discord (Vinick and Ekerdt, 1989). Couples should be supported in the idea that the first year of retirement can be, should be, and usually is a gratifying time of life.

References

Albrecht, T.L., & Adelman, M.B. 1984. Social support and life stress: New directions for communication research. *Human Communication Research,* 11:3–32.

Blau, Z.S. 1973. *Old age in a changing society.* New York: New Viewpoints.

Ekerdt, D.J. 1987. The Normative Aging Study. *Encyclopedia of Aging.* In G.L. Maddox, et al. (Eds.) New York: Springer.

Vinick, B.H., & Ekerdt, D.J. 1989. Retirement and the family. *Generations,* 13:53–57.

Dr. Vinick is a research associate with the VA Normative aging study in Boston, Massachusetts. He is associate director of the Center on Aging at the University of Kansas Medical Center, Kansas City, Missouri.

Husbands and Wives in Retirement: Differences in Needs for Personal Freedom, Space, Privacy

by Gail S. Eisen, Ph.D.

These are highlights of a recent University of Michigan doctoral dissertation investigating changes in the marital relationships and life at home for retired men and their wives.

Study participants included 112 men and women, consisting of 56 couples in which the husband had retired from a full-time occupation within the previous 6 to 20 months. The sample was drawn from male retirees of five large organizations in Michigan and California.

Research methodology for this project combined both quantitative and qualitative elements: a self-administered survey was used in conjunction with extensive personal interviews for each participant, yielding a wealth of information about couples' adaptation to retirement.

Results of this study suggest that men and women may inhabit different spatial and psychological cultures within the retirement household.

Distinct gender differences were discovered in relation to changes in personal freedom, the quality of personal time, requirements for personal space and privacy and level of activity. Women overwhelmingly described decreased freedom, disruption of personal routines, a shrinking of both physical and social space, and activity constriction relative to men.

A majority of both husbands and wives reported participating in more activities as a couple in retirement, with women expressing negative reactions to shared activities at rates consistently higher than men. Men were more likely than women to report that retirement had posed no real problems for them, but when problems were identified, husbands and wives tended to see their problems as rooted in different sources.

Consistently, the same reality was experienced differently, on topics ranging from perceptions of time and its passage to evaluations of spatial rearrangements in the home since the time of retirement, to the content of pre-retirement course materials presented by the employer before the onset of retirement.

Results of this investigation suggest greater attention be given to family and relationship topics in retirement education programs. We have developed curriculum design materials, intervention techniques and seminars suitable for corporate and academic pre-retirement planning programs based upon this study.

Dr. Eisen is a Gerontology Consultant in Los Angeles, California.

Sexuality Continues to Be Important in Later Years

by Richard A. Kaye

We are living in a time when society seems increasingly tolerant of sexual self-determination for virtually every segment of the population. Why then, do we still cling to outdated morality and ideas when we consider the sexuality of older men and women?

In this article, I will examine some myths and cultural attitudes that perpetuate these views. Then, I'll review research studies that deal with the effects of aging on sexual functioning and barriers to sexuality. I will end with a plea for education.

Myths and Cultural Attitudes

The myths about aging are many. In the area of human sexuality and the elderly, myths are not only rampant, they are believed by young, middle aged, and unfortunately, by the elderly themselves.

Older people adopt a negative view of their own sexual desires, fantasies and feelings. In other words, the myth of sexless older years held by young people becomes a self-fulfilling prophecy when they themselves have reached old age. Many elderly people who find they have sexual desires are overwhelmed with guilt and shame and feel that they are oversexed.

The fact that men and women are interested in sex and participate in a variety of sexual activities in their 70s, 80s, and beyond astonishes many people young and old. A significant segment of our society assumes that older people do not have any sexual desires, and are unable to do anything sexually even if they wanted to; are physically unattractive, and therefore sexually undesirable; are fragile physically and might harm themselves; or that any sexual activity in old age is perverse.

Frequently the victims of jokes, elderly men are often ridiculed as "impotent" or as "dirty old men." At 20, these men were described as "virile" but at 60 they are "lecherous." Older women, on the other hand, are considered to have gone through a metamorphosis from sexy young things to being mature and sexually interesting, but with the arrival of age 50, decline into sexual oblivion.

Culturally derived stereotypes, fostered by negative attitudes toward the aging, contribute to the prevailing resistance to accepting the sexuality of older people. In the 1960s and 1970s, many of these values were formalized in institutional practices that went along with the stereotypical treatment of the older patient or resident regarding sexual matters.

Commonly, nursing homes or institutions for the aged restricted contact between the sexes to public lounges so that the residents' behavior could more easily be supervised. Even married residents were often separated! Few, if any admission forms asked any questions about sexuality and most professional journals and books discussing the management of nursing homes ignored the subject.

Any display of sexuality was and still is, viewed with horror by many, or embarrassment, and often leads to further segregation. Certainly, these practices further encourage feelings of guilt and/or abnormality, hindering normal sexual relationships among the elderly.

Under current guidelines for many nursing homes, only married residents are assured privacy for visits by the spouse and are permitted to share a room unless indicated otherwise by the attending physician.

Other common myths about the elderly and sexuality are: sexual desire ceases with menopause; sex is only for the young; older widows and spinsters are sexless; menopausal women need to take hormones to stay sexually interested or active; the "change of life" makes women crabby; and impotence in older men cannot be treated.

Sexual activity in older people is generally though of as taboo; almost second to incest. However, sexuality is a function of one's total personality and encompasses one's value system, lifestyle, self-image, style of communication, gender, biological role, hormonal role, chromosomal role, social role, etc. Sexuality encompasses all of who we are as human beings and how we feel about all of this.

The need for caring, sharing, loving and intimacy begins very early in human development and continues throughout one's life. This need is not banished from human personality and behavior as a person ages. On the contrary, the reality of a "significant other" or "intimate other" may be more critical in the older years when meaningful relationships are fewer, as friends and relatives move away or die and loneliness becomes inevitable. The need for touch and affection is extremely important for the aged individual.

Research Studies

Studies have adequately documented that sexual desire, interest and activity may continue into the ninth decade of life. This is certainly far later than generally assumed. While it is true that sexual interest and activity decrease with advancing years, cessation is most often found to be a result of a decline in the physical health of one or both partners.

The most significant research about sex and aging has been documented in four major studies: (1) Alfred Kinsey and his associates, who studied sexual behavior among the aged; (2) Eric Pfeiffer and his colleagues whose longitudinal study of aging adults supported the Kinsey data and gave more information about sexual activity; (3) Masters and Johnson's research, which provided the first valid information on the physiological changes of sex among the aging; and (4) the Starr-Weiner Report, whose respondents reported on effective responses of their sexual experiences.

Kinsey's findings began to challenge the myth that sexuality terminates naturally in later life. At age 60, most of Kinsey's male subjects were sexually capable and little evidence of sexual decline was found in females until very late in life. Kinsey indicated that individuals with high levels of sexual activity in their younger years were more likely to continue sexual activities as they aged.

Longitudinal studies by Eric Pfeiffer examined 250 people between the ages of 60 and 94 every 3 years for more than 20 years. Findings indicated that interest in sexual intercourse was common and that individual patterns of interest differed greatly among both males and females. What occurred in this sampling over a period of time was not a decline in sexual interest but a growing discrepancy between interest and activity.

The study found a large number of variables influencing the sexual behavior of men as compared with women. Increased age, antihypertensive drugs, cardiovascular medication, declining health and anxiety about upcoming physical examinations had measurable negative effects.

Past sexual interest, sexual enjoyment and sexual frequency—three indicators of early sexual life function—correlated positively with present sexual interests and activity among men and women. For women, however, current sexual interest and activity were more dependent upon marital status. This finding confirmed previous observations that, among elderly women, the presence of an interested able mate is not always enough. Optimally, he also needs to be her marriage partner.

The Masters and Johnson research revealed that men and women in generally good health are physiologically able to have a satisfying sex life well into their 70s and beyond. Individuals who, during their youth and middle age retained their sexual vigor and interest, would continue to do so into old age. The most prevalent cause of sexual dysfunction in the aging male is not physiological but socio-cultural in nature; performance anxiety and the fear of failure. According to Masters and Johnson, both sexes are influenced in their sexual behavior more significantly by the prevailing attitudes and information they have about sex and about the consequences of desexualization that they come to feel within themselves.

In the Starr-Weiner Report, the study was based on how aging adults feel about sexual activities in which they did or did not participate. Findings indicate that "older people seem to define and express their sexuality in more diffuse and varied terms; they seem to be less goal-oriented in their sexual expressions; and they often perceive a sexual experience less in qualifying terms and more in the significance and quality of that experience."

Effects of Aging on Sexual Functioning

The Male

At ages 60, 70, and 80, the male reproductive system is different in form and function than what it was at ages 20 and 50. As with other aspects of normal aging, reduced sexual functioning does not mean an absence of activity.

Hormone production and testosterone output continues into old age. Though testosterone in men is available at a higher level for longer periods of time than estrogen is in women, the amount is increasingly inadequate and affects the genital tissues as aging progresses. A gradual decline in sexual energy, muscle strength and viable sperm result from this hormone depletion. The testes become smaller and less firm; seminiferous tubules (where sperm are produced) thicken and begin a degenerative process which finally inhibits the production of sperm. As the prostate gland enlarges, its contractions become weaker. There is a reduction in volume and viscosity of seminal fluid and the ejaculatory force decreases. No one of these changes is a major event, but together they are responsible for some very real and apparent changes in the total expression of male sexuality.

According to Masters and Johnson, as a male ages (60 and over) speed of attaining an erection, intensity of sensation, frequency of intercourse and the force of ejaculation are reduced to a certain degree; and depending on the individual, each of the four phases of the human sexual response cycle—excitement, plateau, orgasm and resolution—depart from the youthful pattern. The most characteristic change is an increase in the time involved in each phase. Studies indicate that the changes in aged men are quantitative rather than qualitative when compared with younger men.

An advantage of age is that, generally speaking, ejaculatory control is far better among older men than it is in younger men. Because arousal is slower, the older man is likely to engage in sexual foreplay, I term it "pleasuring," as this term often reduces the anxiety about subsequent sexual intercourse. Since foreplay precedes intercourse, one might assume foreplay must lead to intercourse.

By using the term "pleasuring," we can pleasure each other without being pressured to engage in intercourse at a more leisurely pace. During penetration, older men are liberated from the ejaculatory urgency that younger men often display. Older men have had more time to overcome their sexual inhibition and have gained skill in lovemaking.

The Female

Physiologically, the older woman seems to experience little sexual difficulty. According to Masters and Johnson, "There is no time limit drawn by advancing years to female sexuality." If moderate good health, a good positive attitude toward sex and an available effective partner prevail, sexual activity can extend until the very late years, 90 and beyond.

The Masters and Johnson studies show that the principle physical changes in the aging women are caused by the decline of estrogen and progesterone after menopause. The vaginal wall atrophies and becomes less elastic and the vagina shortens and narrows. Approximately five years after menopause, the rate and quality of vaginal mucous secretions during sexual arousal are also reduced. Consequently, intercourse may be painful for older women.

Sexual intercourse in women of any age may lead to a urinary tract infection, but it is more prominent in the older woman since the atrophic bladder and urethra are more susceptible to irritation and are not protected by the thinning vagina.

As women age, both the duration and intensity of the physiological responses to sexual stimulation diminish gradually. Consequently, older women need more and longer stimulation during sexual activity. Despite these physiological changes, the four phases of the human sexual response cycle can still be experienced.

According to Kinsey et al., there is no falling off in sexual arousability with advancing years; frequently there is an increase. Most menopausal and post-menopausal women maintain the multiorgasmic capability of their younger years, particularly if they are in good general health and receive regular effective sexual stimulation.

Barriers to Sexuality

If research and statistics prove that active sexual interest and capacity exist in the elderly, then what factors are there that contribute to the dysfunctional, sexless, impotent image of the person over 65? They tend to be the same factors that would affect sexuality and the whole person at any age. The work done by Masters and Johnson with older men led the researchers to describe six different factors which were responsible for the loss of sexual responsiveness:

1. Monotony of a repetitious sexual relationship (usually translated into boredom with the partner.)
2. Preoccupation with career or economic pursuits.
3. Mental or physical fatigue.
4. Overindulgence in food or drink.
5. Physical and mental infirmities of either partner.
6. Fear of unsatisfactory sexual performance which could result from any of the above.

Among the factors that may contribute to performance anxiety in the older male are slower response times, less frequent and less forceful ejaculations and irregular patterns of orgasm. A single incident of impotence may so seriously alarm an older man that he is discouraged from other attempts.

Furthermore, he may interpret this one experience as a sign of sexual decline due to aging. Another factor that may contribute to impotence is a prolonged illness in either partner.

It is important to note that more than 80% of men who had prostatectomies and 70% or women who had hysterectomies retain potency and coital enjoyment.

A Need for Education; A Plea for Education

Obviously there is a great need for education about sexuality among the aging. Educators and health professionals are in a good position to assume responsibility of educating the young and the old. Professionals with a fundamental grasp of anatomy and physiology of normal aging are ideal persons to disseminate accurate information, and encourage attitudinal change. Information should be given to the aged themselves, as well as families, friends and misinformed peers.

A critical step in helping older individuals maintain their sexuality or overcome sexual problems is to obtain a data base on their educational, economic and cultural background; previous level of sexual activity; previous methods of sexual expression, and the importance of continued sexual activity. To conduct an interview that elicits this information, professionals must be aware of their own feelings, attitudes, values and comfort level regarding sexual matters.

The presentation of basic sex education and the effects of the aging process on sexuality is another step. This is especially important for older men who fear permanent impotence due to the occasional failure of attaining an erection. When both partners understand the normal changes that occur with age, neither partner will mistake such changes for the loss of sexuality. The increased importance of foreplay (pleasuring) with advancing age should be explained, and the partners encouraged to explore the pleasures of holding, touching and caressing each other. Manual stimulation of the genitals can be suggested as well as having sexual intercourse in the morning or after taking a nap if one or both partners tire easily.

A recommendation to avoid sexual activity after a heavy meal or overindulgence in alcohol is essential because potency is affected by both. Above all, partners are urged to communicate to each other about what is pleasing and satisfying to them.

Since some chronic diseases, even though stabilized, may interfere directly or indirectly with one's health, it is a factor that can affect one's sexuality. Specific information must be provided concerning capacities and limitations of sexual activity related to any existing health condition. For the patient with arthritis, for example, the professional might suggest position changes for intercourse to lessen pain in given joints. If medication is taken that diminishes sexual drives, patients need to report this change to their physician.

Elderly men, particularly those with chronic conditions such as cardiovascular disease, need special instructions because prolonged abstinence may impede the resumption of sexual activity. The length of the time after a heart attack before a man or woman can engage in sexual activity should be discussed with a physician. Generally, sexual activity is resumed gradually.

At all stages of life, human beings need to be loved and nurtured by other responsive humans. The aged too are human beings; and they too seek to satisfy their need for caring, affection, love and sex; enjoying these expressions as much as possible within the framework of their mental and physiological capabilities.

Knowledge and renewed sensitivity on the part of all educators and caregivers can help the elderly realize their full potential for sexual enjoyment and eradicate the myths that exist regarding sexuality and the aged.

Richard A. Kaye is a Professor of Health Education at Kingsborough Community College of The City University of New York.

6

EARLY RETIREMENT/ DOWNSIZING

Early Retirement—Policy Issues and Trends

Government's Short-Term and Long-Term Policies Are in Conflict, and No One's Attempting to Reconcile Them

by Prof. Leonard Stitelman, Ph.D.

As we approach the tweny-first Century, it is startling to consider the shifts in attitudes in our society toward the concept of retirement. I will briefly review these changes, and then consider some public policy issues and trends surrounding retirement, with particular focus on the nature of "early retirement."

Retirement as a specific stage of life was virtually unknown in the first one hundred years following the Declaration of Independence.

Andrew Achenbaum developed this history in his outstanding book, "Old Age in the New Land." He points out that the first edition of Webster's "American Dictionary" in 1828 defined the word "retirement" with no application to older people.

Thus, the idea that an employee at a specific age automatically stopped working was absent from the definition of the word. Achenbaum reports that "no profession, industry, business, craft, or trade organization prior to 1860 required people to leave the labor force because they had reached a predetermined chronological age."

It was not surprising that early Americans chose as the new nation's image and spirit a "sinewy old man with long white hair and chin whiskers." Uncle Sam caught the character of all ages.

The Industrial Revolution following the Civil War marks the watershed shift to retirement, but it was unfortunately connected with factories and blue collar employees who were readily discarded by management as early as age 40, to be replaced by young people who would work as they were told.

The employee was merely an extension of a machine, and as expendable as a worn out piece of equipment.

Now, Webster's 1880 edition of "American Dictionary" attributes a new meaning to "retire" as "to designate as no longer qualified for active service," and "to give pension to, on account of old age, or other infirmity."

As private industry and the federal government developed policies for discharged employees whose only problem was that they were considered too old to stay on the job, youth, not age, became the focus for advancing society.

When the economic system broke down in 1929 and led us into the most disastrous depression in American history, the response was the establishment of the social welfare responsibility at the national government level.

Although emergency and temporary assistance agencies dominated the Roosevelt New Deal, one permanent agency was approved by Congress in 1935—the Social Security Administration.

The irony of this event is that while it filled a need in our society, it also formalized the principle that old age was itself a problem demanding wholesale government intervention.

It demonstrated that for the first time in American history, a majority of people over age 65 were dependent. It established an institutional structure to assist the elderly.

Current Status of Retirement

Are we now returning to the earliest American tradition described by Achenbaum?

Congress has eliminated the mandatory chronological retirement age for most employment situations.

However, the benefits and payments of Social Security continue on a chronological age basis.

Thus, in the 1980s we see the convergence of better physical health, longer life expectancy, a beckoning leisure industry and the fruits of Social Security system payments.

So here we have the interesting dichotomy—we can continue with full time paid employment as long as we can perform the job, but many of us are opting to leave the workplace as early as financially possible. Of course these are generalities.

Yes, there are many Americans who are productive and stay in the work force into their '70s, '80s, and '90s. But the statistical trend is the reverse.

For many of us, the availability of Social Security payments, a company pension plan and significant personal savings lead to the fact that our society also deals with the issues and problems of what is identified as "early retirement."

Rather than the issues of our brief "declining years," we find that the retirement period can easily include a period of time in our lives of 25 to 40 or more years.

Rather than the issues of our death or dying, we find that the retirement period can easily be dominated by a positive, active, vigorous and exciting lifestyle.

One response to this basic change has been the creation of the International Society for Retirement Planning, which confirms a new profession of individuals who offer counsel, training or assistance to those preparing for retirement.

Early Retirement Policy Issues

Let us review the current usage of "retirement" and "early retirement."

According to the General Accounting Office (GAO), "retirement" is defined as receipt of a pension. It does not imply that a pension recipient is not working for a new employer. "Early retirement" involves both having a pension and leaving the labor force before age 65.

The GAO study reports that 65 no longer appears to be the retirement age chosen by most Americans with private pensions; 62 is the median retirement age. "Most people choose to retire before age 65," states the GAO, and notes that most private plans allow employees to retire as early as age 55 with reduced benefits.

It should be mentioned that the majority of early pension recipients are not receiving disability benefits. The need to address this policy issue is reinforced by the report that retirement before age 65 is a trend noted since the early 1970s.

Although several factors lead to early retirement, most analysts focus on the increasing availability and attendant encouragement of "early-out" plans.

Both the public and private sectors are using these incentives to reduce the numbers and costs of their work force. The primary targets are middle-level managers in their fifties whose salaries afford the greatest immediate monetary savings, particularly for corporations concerned with cash flow.

As various retirement plans evolved, both private and public employers have added incentives to encourage early retirement.

The following is an outline of the reasons for such encouragement:

a. Need to reduce the work force in declining industries,

b. Need to reduce the work force in times of economic downturn,

c. Need to provide promotion opportunities for younger employees, particularly women and minority group members,

d. Need to avoid legal challenges to forced retirement or termination,

e. Reduce compensation and fringe benefit costs,

f. Interest in maintaining a balanced age structure in the organization,

g. Employee preferences.

The basic policy issue that has emerged comes from the fact that economic incentives in private and public plans to retire early, combined with the size of the pension, are major determinants of the retirement decision.

The early retirement trend must be evaluated in conjunction with increasing life expectancy.

Congress has been dealing with the public policy elements of this subject. The general attitude is one of concern.

In 1983 amendments to the Social Security Act, receipt of full retirement benefits will gradually increase from 65 to 67.

Thus, an employee retiring at age 62 will see a 30 percent reduction, compared with the current 20 percent benefit reduction. While age 65 today sees no reduction, a 13 percent reduction will occur under the new rules.

Employees also face forced early retirement because of reorganization and restructuring of the bureaucracy.

It is estimated that more than one million professionals, white collar managers and technicians have been terminated early by either route. A General Accounting Office report found that of first time Social Security beneficiaries in 1980 and 1981, 76 percent of the men and 84 percent of the women were under age 65.

Retirement planners now face the reality that most employees retiring today will live well into the twenty-first Century.

Conclusion

The basic policy conflict may center around short term versus long term goals. As was described earlier, both private and public employers are offering incentives for early retirement. Employees are responding positively in increasing numbers, thus permitting the accomplishment of short term goals (e.g., reduce payrolls).

However, there is a long term goal already in place of encouraging people to work longer (e.g., elimination of mandatory retirement age).

There is little indication that our governmental policy bodies are attempting to reconcile or bring consistency out of this conflict.

Perhaps the 1990s will see an emphasis on transition formats, or flexible work options, a concept bridging the current practice of traditional full time employee today—full time retiree tomorrow. Examples of work modifications already in place in very limited situations include:

- Part-time reemployment

- Phased or gradual retirement

- Consultant

- Seasonal reemployment

- Job sharing

- Retiree job pools for peak period work

- Flextime

- Emeritus positions

Meanwhile, it is to the credit of organizations such as AARP, and professional groups such as American Society on Aging, that the human element of the individual needs brought about by society's short term goals, are being addressed. The resolution of public policy conflicts regarding early retirement should be considered a very high priority in the next decade.

Sources

AARP News, "Changes in Business Climate Reshape Retirement Issues," February 1988, pp. 1, 12.

Achenbaum, Andrew, *Old Age in the New Land,* Johns Hopkins Press, 1978.

Feurer, Dale, "Retirement Planning: A Coming Imperative," *Training,* February 1985, pp. 49–53.

General Accounting Office, *Pensions Plans,* August 1987.

General Accounting Office, *Retirement Before Age 65 Is a Growing Trend in the Private Sector,* July 15, 1985.

General Accounting Office, *Retirement Before Age 65—Trends, Costs and National Issues,* July 1986.

Goddard, Robert, "How to Harness America's Gray Power," *Personnel Journal,* May 1987, pp. 33–40.

Hubbartt, William, "The Growing Controversy Over Retirement," *Office Administration and Automation,* October 1983, pp. 35–37.

Second Annual Special on Retirement Planning, *Aging Network News,* January 1987.

Watts, Patti, "Preretirement Planning: Making the Golden Years Rosy," *Personnel,* March 1987, pp. 32–39.

Dr. Stitelman is Professor of Public Administration at the University of New Mexico, Albuquerque, New Mexico.

Downsizing . . . Early Retirement Incentives . . . and Pre-Retirement Education

by Charles M. Atwell

Many companies are reducing their workforce in an effort to reduce costs. They are trimming "excess" workers and layers of management to improve overall profitability. Companies are using various strategies that will be reviewed in this report.

Most companies want to avoid layoffs and involuntary terminations that can result in demoralizing the remaining workforce and/or legal pitfalls. They want to downsize their workforce on a voluntary basis. Encouraging people to take voluntary separation through resignations, early retirement and retirement can be accomplished in several ways:

a. Resignation bonuses

b. Offering early retirement benefits at age 50 or 55

c. Offering early retirement incentives such as added years of service, years of age or both

d. Offering training and education programs on early retirement and pre-retirement planning.

Let's look at how the workforce is changing and how the needs of employers and employees can be achieved through planning.

Overview

The demographics of the American workforce are changing dramatically. The labor force of older workers as a whole has decreased steadily and this is expected to continue.

Historically, when employees reached age 65, they were expected to retire and receive their ceremonial gold watch. Times have changed since passage of anti-discrimination laws. The needs of industry have also changed due to technology, robotics, etc.

Many large corporations are trying to downsize. For example, companies such as Reliance Electric Co. will hire only enough to replace those departing. "We're trying to do more with the same resources." Olin Corp. expects only "selective replacement at all levels."[1]

Downsizing and selective replacement are particularly significant to older employees who want to continue or feel they need to continue working. The older population (persons 65 years or older) numbered 29.2 million in 1986. They represented 12.1% of the U.S. population, or about one in every eight Americans. People are living longer. In 1986, persons reaching age 65 had an average life expectancy of an additional 16.9 years according to the Administration on Aging (AOA).[2]

Working at a job to age 65 and retiring to a rocking chair is a myth. Nearly 70% of those people filing for Social Security benefits do so before age 65, and 50% file at 62. Some early retirement programs offered by employers start monthly benefits at age 55 to provide income until Social Security begins payment at age 62. This is referred to as "leveling."

Downsizing

Reduction of the number of workers and layers of management is a major concern of large companies. The American Management Association surveyed 353 people at the 1987 Human Resource Conference and found 22% planned to reduce their workforces and 30% expect to initiate or expand cutbacks in the near future. Only 14.2% of those surveyed report their companies offer job re-training programs.[3]

The AMA also polled 1,134 companies and found 515 or 45.5% have reduced their workforce, with 210 more companies planning to do so in the next few years. As published in "MANAGEMENT REVIEW,"[4] Eric Rolfe Greenberg, Project Director for the AMA, said "The survey reveals that downsizing is no longer 'just' a reaction to the economy because it takes place during good economic periods and bad.... Two thirds of the companies that have downsized consider themselves well prepared for another round of belt tightening, while less than half the firms that have done no recent downsizing believe they are prepared." According to the survey, manufacturing firms have been hit harder than service related ones, 57% of the manufacturers in the sample reported downsizing as compared to 37% of service providers.

Respondents were given a checklist of services that companies often provided to discharged workers, ranging from early retirement incentives, which proved the most popular tactic, through job redeployment plans and benefit extensions to renegotiation of union contracts. According to this survey only 11.9% of the companies offered personal financial counseling. "Respondents' ratings of the benefits realized from outplacement services reflect corporate concern with the morale and productivity of the remaining workforce and with public opinion in the affected community."

The "Management Review"[4] quoted Neil Redford, president of the Redford Group, a New York-based executive outplacement firm, "There is a good side to downsizing," he explained, "People get up, dust themselves off, and often go on to better positions. Managers reevaluate their lives and end up leading a happier existence."

Dealing with Downsizing

While IBM, Hewlett Packard and others encourage voluntary employee reduction through bonuses and incentives, other employers use involuntary layoffs as a solution to downsizing. Some employers have developed their own alternatives to downsizing through training and education.

Many companies are trying to deal with the issue. Unfortunately the newness of the problem means there is much to be learned about dealing with the problem of downsizing. Let's look at what is being done.

Retraining and Education

Retraining and education of the workforce is an alternative to downsizing. Ms. Nell Eilrich, an educational consultant at the Carnegie Foundation for the Advancement of Teaching, estimates that U.S. companies are currently spending upward of $40 billion a year to deliver education to 8 million workers, as reported in "MANAGEMENT REVIEW".[3]

"At Motorola Inc.'s training and education center in Schaumburg, Illinois, . . . engineers prepare for exams that could lead to a master's degree in computer science. Next door, middle-aged managers explore 'just in time' strategies resupplying inventories. Across the hall, clerical workers learn techniques to increase their typing speed. Motorola spent two years re-tooling its mechanical engineers—where skills are less vital to a growing high-technology company—for jobs as electrical engineers. They want to gain the competitive edge . . . with more broadly educated workers."

Downsizing is particularly painful for many older workers. While the number of early retirement offers increases, many workers are not prepared financially or psychologically to elect early retirement. More companies are now beginning to offer educational pre-retirement programs to better prepare older workers for retirement. Others are retraining employees.

Early Retirement Benefits

According to the "1987 Top 50 Wyatt Survey," employees age 55 with 25 years service could receive an average of 71% of their accrued benefits, those aged 55 with 30 years could receive 78% and employees aged 60 with 30 years of service 96% of their accrued benefits.[5] Early retirement benefits are available to anyone who reaches the required age and years of service with the employer.

The next most popular downsizing offer is early retirement incentives added to the early retirement benefits such as adding years of service and/or years of age to determine early retirement benefits during the offering period.

Early Retirement Offers

A survey of the salaried pension plans of the top 50 industrial employers in the U.S. conducted by the Wyatt Company[5] found that 16 of the companies offered early retirement "windows" in 1986, compared to only six in 1985. In the last 10 years, 30 of the 50 companies extended such offers, 15 of them more than once. The survey also found that the number of post-retirement benefit increases had dropped in the last several years, since reaching a high point in 1981.[5] Benefits had been escalating due to higher inflation rates.

The Wyatt survey of the 30 companies which offered an early 'retirement window,' 20 reported a 'window' period of one to three months, with half of the companies reporting two months. The longest 'window' period reported was three years and the shortest one day.

When early retirement incentives are offered their acceptance varies widely.

It depends in large measure on the offer made and the number of eligible employees. Because of possible tax repercussions, 50 year olds and 55 year olds will differ significantly in their acceptance rates when offered 5 years of service and 5 years of age. Separation from service following attainment of age 55 qualifies as an "early retirement exception" not subject to 10% excise penalty tax but subject to income tax if not rolled over into an IRA within 60 days. Knowledge is a factor.

Acceptance of retirement incentives is significantly higher among those employees who have had pre-retirement education.

Early Retirement Incentives

While it is too early to report on the incidence of early retirement incentives for calendar year 1987, indications are that there was an increase from that of previous years. "Spencer's Survey"[6] did a random sampling of employer subscribers in 1987 and 189 responses were received. It was learned that 23.8%, or 45 employers, offered early retirement incentives in 1986. The most frequent eligibility requirements were age 55 with 10 or more years of service. The Spencer survey on early retirement incentives for 1986 showed a significant rise in the incidence of incentives for 1986 over prior years. Enhanced early retirement rose from 7.6% in 1984 to 23.8% in 1986 for those employers responding to the survey. Nearly all (39 of 45) of the offering employers targeted this incentive at employees in their fifties.

AT&T's Experience

Since AT&T's divestiture of the Bell Companies, incentive early retirement programs have been initiated to reduce expenses. The divestiture represented a break with the traditional AT&T lifetime job guarantee. The 1984 break-up resulted in massive overstaffing as they entered an era of competition. One of the Bell companies is Southern New England Telecommunications (SNET).

Southern New England Telecommunications

The "Wall Street Journal" reported that SNET[7] offered early retirement to 4,300 managers in September 1987. They reported that 572 managers accepted the offer. Among incentives being offered was the addition of 5 years to their service with the company for the purpose of determining benefits for those retiring before December 31, 1987. They also offered to add five years to the effective age of managers who were too young to qualify for the normal minimum age for retirement benefits. This is known as the "5 and 5" Early Retirement Incentive which is among the sweetest early retirement offers.

Walter H. Montieth, Jr., Chairman and Chief Executive Officer of SNET said in the October 30, 1987 quarterly report, "We will be well positioned to reduce expenses through a smaller management workforce. These measures together with our cost reduction efforts will make SNET a leaner, stronger and ultimately a more successful company."

Who Are the Early Retirees?

Industrial psychologists at AT&T "found that managers who accepted early retirement viewed life and work quite differently from those who stayed." The "Wall Street Journal" reported the researchers found three types of characteristics which distinguished early retirees from those who remained: work motivation and attitudes, personal values, interests and financial feasibility. The biggest gap between the early retirees and those who stayed was displayed in an attitude called identification.

The active group was much more likely to feel part of the management team than the early retirees. The early retirees were a fun-loving group, more involved in such leisure time pursuits as hobbies, sports, partying and socializing. The early retirees had fewer financial worries and less need for a secure job.

The study found the market value of their homes, for instance, was $74,000 more than the value of the homes owned by the managers who remained.

Ms. Ann Howard, a former AT&T psychologist who headed the research, noted that, "companies, by conducting periodic attitude surveys, conceivably could identify potential early retirees and target incentives to them." Most of the retired workers interviewed spoke positively about their careers and employer.[8]

After the incentive for early retirement is offered and accepted, offers to re-hire select former employees as consultants or engage them through sub-contractors may be made by the former employer. Employers do need to be careful in their offer of early retirement and/or to rehire, however.

Selective Retirement Planning

The federal Age Discrimination in Employment Act (ADEA) prohibits discrimination against nearly all people age 40 and older. About 33 state and local governments have passed similar laws against age discrimination. Though the ADEA is the preeminent law in cases of employment discrimination, if a state or local law provides greater protection, the state or local law takes precedence over the ADEA.

Early retirement incentives can be a means to avoid the age discrimination issues but cannot be offered on a selective or discriminatory basis to only certain employees.

When companies offer early retirement incentives to their employees some key employees (MVPs) may elect to receive early retirement benefits. A select few of these employees may be contacted subsequent to their decision to accept early retirement and be offered personal consulting positions with the same employer.

Companies who re-hire select employees as consultants are very cautious in handling early retirement offerings. Some people might suggest that this is selective retirement planning. Other companies such as the operating telecommunication companies engage the services of contractors. Contractors recruit and hire employees who have elected early retirement in order that they can go back to their former employer under an employment arrangement with the contractor.

Facilitating Early Retirement

How can employers facilitate early retirement planning? Since more employees are now planning for their own retirement, the most effective method is to offer pre-retirement training and educational seminars and workshops.

Potential retirees have several probable areas of discomfort with the question of retirement. These areas include financial questions, lifestyle, adjustments and psychological considerations.

Facing these issues and addressing solutions, in order to make employees comfortable with the transition to 'retirement' is the goal of pre-retirement training.

Retirement Income Needs

In pre-retirement training, issues and concerns of the participants must be identified and addressed. For example, if a person is contemplating retirement, how much income will be necessary to maintain a person's present or expected lifestyle? According to the Executive Director of the American Association of Retired Persons, "Adequate income is a key factor in preparing for successful retirement. The goal should be to maintain at least 75% of the income earned before retirement. If you are earning $20,000 per year, you should have $15,000 a year in retirement income from pensions, social security benefits, and other assets." He added, "Too many people plan on retirement who do not have adequate income."

Most financial planners recommend one-half to two-thirds of a person's current income as an objective for retirement planning. The children have usually completed their formal education and the mortgage is usually paid off or nearly paid off. Changes in lifestyle frequently influence a person's income needs. Financial planning prior to

and subsequent to retirement has to be monitored on a regular basis.

Comprehensive Financial Planning

The retirement income need is just one of the issues that must be addressed in comprehensive pre-retirement financial planning. The other needs are risk management-life insurance, disability insurance, auto insurance, Medicare supplement, etc.; sufficient cash reserves for emergencies and opportunities; tax planning for pre- and post-retirement such as reduction of taxes, using IRA's if deductible or non-deductible since they can earn on a tax deferred basis; investment planning is important so that appropriate investment vehicles are used.

A major question for pre-retirees is, "Do I rollover my retirement plan distribution(s) into an IRA?"

The alternatives are taking distribution before age 55 and paying an income tax plus a 10% excise penalty tax, or at age 55 or older and paying the income tax subject to five year forward averaging, 10 year forward averaging, or possibly capital gains tax. If the distribution(s) are rolled over into an IRA—no current tax is payable and the entire amount continues to grow on a tax deferred basis until taken out. The payout must start by age 70½ and is taxed as ordinary income when paid out to the retiree.

Other financial needs are the development of financial statements, a balance sheet, an income statement, plus a cash flow and budget analysis. Most people have not developed financial statements but must do so in planning for retirement. For example, one early retiree who participated in a workshop said, "As soon as I have 50% of my working income, I am going to retire." He planned for 5 years, reached the 50% objective and now he and his wife love their retirement. They also love to share their success with other pre-retirees in workshops on pre-retirement planning.

Estate Planning

Everyone has an estate. Most, unfortunately, do not have a plan.

If a person names their spouse as beneficiary of their retirement plans, then the surviving spouse can rollover the distribution into an IRA without any current tax. This is only available to a surviving spouse.

The estate planning attorney will review such issues as wills, trusts, both living and testamentary and the reasons why living wills, durable power of attorney and other legal issues are important in retirement planning. Making gifts to children, grandchildren, loved ones, charities and non-profits are part of estate planning.

Employees Responsibilities

Most workers now believe they must provide for their own retirement, according to a recent nationwide survey released by the Employers Council on Flexible Compensation (ECFC). The survey, conducted by Opinion Research Corp. asked over 1,000 Americans who they felt was responsible for retirement savings. Responses indicated a perceived shift in this responsibility from the federal government and employers to the individual. Five years ago, only 38% of the American public felt the individual was responsible for retirement income. That figure has now risen to 53% according to Ken Feltman, Executive Director of ECFC.[9] The publicity given IRA's, thrift savings plans, 401(K)s and others has given impetus to this development.

Of those employees interviewed, 41% participated in pension plans at work. Participation dropped somewhat in other related company-sponsored programs.

Participation in available retirement options varies according to education levels and income, according to a survey reported by the Research Institute of America's "Employment Alert."

We can help these employees continue to develop a greater sense of responsibility by helping them develop their own short-term and long-term retirement planning.

Short-Term Planning

A Special Report, "Firm Footing for Your Retirement" in the January, 1988 issue of "Money" noted that some 49 million American workers are tied to Wall Street through company-sponsored pension plans. The vast majority of them never thought of themselves as stock market investors.[10]

After the market drop, October 19, 1987, many employers realized that by retiring before the end of October they could still redeem their pummeled stock fund holdings at their much higher September 30 prices. "Money" gave an example of what happened next. At Lockheed 600 employees retired in October, twice the expected number, and New York City public schools lost 272 educators, compared with a usual monthly retirement loss of 100.

This was short-term planning (action or re-action) important nevertheless. Thousands of employees who were considering retirement had to make a decision prior to October 31, 1987, to elect a valuation of September 30, 1987, for their retirement benefits. Retirement planning should be long-term.

Long-Term Planning

In "AFTER THE CRASH: New Financial Planning Approaches," Commerce Clearing House authors Sidney Kess and Bertil Westlin, include a section on "Retirement Planning." Their analysis was that the 1987 crash had dealt a severe blow to many participants in "so-called qualified retirement plans" and IRAs funds heavily invested in equities.

. . . Today . . . when the added TRA-86 pension costs come home to roost, many employers (especially small business employers) are contemplating and some are initiating steps to terminate defined benefit plans. The cutback and elimination of tax-deductible IRA's coupled with the cutback and, in some cases, total elimination of qualified plan benefits, the Crash, Tax Reform Act-86 and costs in social security benefits . . . make it clear that individuals without prospects for large inheritances must undertake to provide their own retirement via extra savings and careful investment, without the aid of the employers or Uncle Sam.

In long-term planning everyone should consider contributing to an IRA even if it is not tax deductible. Another retirement planning consideration is eligibility for thrift or savings plan, profit sharing and company sponsored 401(K) plans.[11]

In "USA Today" Jim Henderson quoted this author as saying, "It's time to come back down to earth, reassess your goals and set up a long-term game plan." People don't plan to fail but many people fail to plan. The smart money is on diversifying . . . back to basics. The objective should be financial security and independence through retirement planning.[12]

Retirement planning starts when a person takes that first job and continues through the last job.

Employers can facilitate employees' retirement planning through training and education.

Pre-retirement Plan

In 1987, Towers, Perrin, Benefit Consultants surveyed the Fortune 1,000 companies.

With 269 companies responding, over 85% strongly agreed that companies should sponsor pre-retirement training. However, only 48% actually offered it and some only offered post-retirement benefits information.[13]

Pre-retirement training is frequently offered to employees age 55 or older although many companies offer it at age 50. A person's pre-retirement training should start at least three to five years before retirement age. It is important to recognize that many individuals have a negative view on the subject of retirement. This negative perception may result in their procrastination in planning for retirement. If retirement is viewed as negative and they do procrastinate then early retirement programs and incentives will be less successful.

Pre-retirement training can change that negative perception to a positive one of a transition to a new lifestyle. Making their transition to retirement requires personal savings and planning for retirement security.

A 1987 "Wall Street Journal" headline reported "Personal Savings rate heads for 40 year low." The article noted that "Blue Chip Financial Forecasts," a Sedona, Arizona newsletter that interviewed 51 forecasters monthly predicts that the personal savings rate in 1988 will fall to 3.6% of disposable income, the lowest level since 1947's 3.1%.[14] That savings rate may be affected by the fluctuations in the stock market and its effect on a spend, spend, spend lifestyle.

Transitions in Retirement

In pre-retirement education one of the most important concepts is that you don't retire "from" a job but retire "to" something. A person participates through self-assessment, identifies individual retirement activities and interests that will offer that participant psychic income and self-fulfillment.

This may mean a new job or career, pure leisure, study, volunteerism, hobbies, avocations, travel or a combination of activities that the participant wants in "retirement." As noted previously those with outside interests, hobbies, and a plan for activities seem to fare best psychologically.

Pre-retirement training usually addresses financial needs. Equally as important are the psychological needs of the employee. For example, most people who are offered incentive early retirement but do not take it have two primary reasons—they don't feel comfortable psychologically and/or don't feel comfortable financially.

Evaluating an Early Retirement Incentive Plan

"Does an information and counseling program help employees facing retirement incentives? Does it help the organization?" Yes, according to the assessment study by Westchester County, New York officials. In a comparison of the same early retirement incentives offered to different groups of county employees, they found an average of 30 to 33% of eligible employees accepted the incentive in comparison to over 44% for Westchester County employees . . . who were offered pre-retirement workshops.

"In addition, the evaluations completed by employees at workshops consistently mentioned that the process of learning about one's options should begin more than six months before a specific incentive plan was offered."[15]

In "A Practical Guide For Retirement Living," Elwood N. Chapman said, "Retirement is a passage from one lifestyle to another. Those who take the voyage seriously and do the right kind of planning usually have a smoother trip—and more fun when they arrive."[16]

Pre-retirement training can improve the acceptance of early retirement as well as incentive early retirement offers. This training should be at least three to five years before expected retirement and reviewed periodically. Some employers offer financial planning as an employee benefit at age 40 and pre-retirement at age 50 with annual updates on changes such as Social Security, taxes, etc.

Retirement Planning is a process of providing wellness in future years. Using the holistic approach to wellness means taking charge of our lives. It includes physical, nutritional, mental, social, spiritual and financial wellness. To achieve Retirement Wellness we must have a plan.

References

1. *Wall Street Journal,* Labor Letter, January 19, 1988.
2. *Administration on Aging* (AOA), U.S. Department of Health and Human Services.
3. *AMA Management Review,* December, 1987.
4. *AMA Management Review,* "The Drive to be Leaner and Meaner," January, 1988.
5. *1987 TOP 50, A Survey of Retirement,* January, 1987 "Thrift, and Profit-Sharing Plans," The Wyatt Company, Research and Information Center, Suite 400, 1850 M Street, N.W., Washington, D.C. 20036
6. *Spencer's Research Reports on Employee Benefits,* "Early Retirement Incentives Offered by 24% of Companies in 1986," 1987 Charles D. Spencer & Associates, Inc.
7. *Wall Street Journal,* December 28, 1987, Southern N.E. Telecommunications.
8. *Wall Street Journal,* September 4, 1987 "AT&T Study Shows Early Retirees."

9. *RIA Employment Coordinator,* April 1986. "Nationwide Survey Shows Americans Don't Count On Social Security For Retirement," ECFC, 1660 L St., N.W., Suite 715, Washington, D.C. 20036

10. *Money,* January, 1988, "Firm Footing For Your Retirement."

11. *AFTER THE CRASH: New Financial Planning Approaches,* by Sidney Kess and Bertil Westlin, Commerce Clearing House, Inc., December 1987.

12. *USA TODAY,* October 26, 1987, Cover Story on Personal Finance.

13. Towers, Perrin, To be published early 1988.

14. *Wall Street Journal,* May 11, 1987. The Outlook-Personal Savings.

15. *Retirement Planning,* Febuary, 1988. Mainstream—The Retirement Institute of Westchester Community College, Valhalla, New York.

16. *Comfort Zones: A Practical Guide for Retirement Living,* Elwood N. Chapman, 1987 Crisp Publications, Los Altos, CA.

Mr. Atwell is Vice President of Waddell & Reed Financial Services, Kansas City, Missouri.

Ten Questions Pre-Retirees Should Ask When Evaluating an Early Retirement Offer

by Mary E. Lee

1. What is your employer offering?

Look at the bottom line of any early retirement offer from your employer. Is your pension based on years of service or a set age? Ask whether your employer offers an early pension or supplemental income to offset the absence of Social Security benefits, which won't begin until you reach age 62.

Are your health and life insurance benefits carried on into retirement? If not, replacing these benefits could be expensive.

A bonus based on years of service or annual salary may be included to cover those years between retirement and age 59.5, when the employee's qualified plan becomes available without the 10 percent tax penalty.

Remember, it's inherently more risky to retire early because you have to make your retirement savings last longer.

2. How can you best use your company benefits?

Don't look to your employer to provide the bulk of your retirement savings. Few corporations generate more than 50 percent of the replacement money individuals need during retirement.

If you are a participant in your employer's pension or profit sharing plan, you may be able to choose to take a lump-sum payment (if available), draw a regular pension check or defer payment.

Before deciding, consider the comfort of a monthly pension check versus an unknown investment return on your lump-sum distribution.

Payouts from qualified retirement plans, such as a 401(K) plan, before age 59.5 are subject to a 10 percent early withdrawal tax penalty. An exception: employers whose plans specifically provide for early retirement at or after age 55. Employees taking early withdrawals from their qualified retirement plans must retire, and be at least 55 years old to avoid the penalty.

3. What lifestyle do you desire?

Although you may have sufficient income to cover day-to-day expenses during retirement, it may not provide the lifestyle you wish.

Your spending habits will change—leisure activities will replace business-related expenses. Develop a sound spending plan that takes into account costs for travel and hobbies, because your enjoyment in retirement may depend on them.

4. Can you afford to retire?

Plan to live on about 80 percent of your current non-disposable income to maintain your current standard of living during retirement.

Figure out how much money you'll need to live 30 years beyond retirement. You may not live that long, but it's better to plan for a long life than to run out of money.

Since investment income will likely finance most of your retirement needs, future inflation and interest rates are key to determining how much money you'll need. As a guideline, inflation has averaged 6 percent

over the past 15 years, while interest rates have averaged 8 percent this century.

5. How much insurance will you need?

Consider the four types of insurance: life, health, disability and property/casualty. Perhaps the most important is health, which might include a policy that covers the cost of nursing home care if a catastrophic illness wipes out your life savings and assets.

Even if you start collecting Social Security benefits at age 62, Medicare benefits under Social Security do not begin until you are 65.

6. What is your tax liability?

Many people incorrectly assume they'll be in a lower tax bracket once they retire. Although you will no longer have to pay Social Security taxes, under the new tax law, 10-year income averaging of lump sum distributions from qualified retirement plans became five-year averaging.

The new five-year formula may be available once only if you're at least age 59.5 when you receive your lump-sum distributions. However, there is a grandfather provision: if you were 50 on or before Jan. 1, 1986, you may use a one-time averaging under the rates in effect when the lump-sum distribution is received. You may use either a five-year averaging or 10-year averaging using 1986 tax rates, even if you're under age 59.5.

7. Should you work after you "retire"?

Some employees accept their firm's attractive early retirement offer but don't intend to stop working. They may not have enough money to retire comfortably or may simply enjoy their careers.

But remember, if you're between ages 62 and 66 and work after retirement, you will lose $1 of Social Security benefits for every $2 you earn over $6,120 annually. If you're age 66 to 70, the limit is $8,400.

8. Is your estate in order?

It's important to have an updated will drawn to ensure proper handling of your assets upon death. You may want to discuss with your tax attorney or accountant potential tax savings that trusts and gifts or the unified tax credit may offer.

9. Are you comfortable managing your own money?

Potential retirees should consider how comfortable they are managing large sums of money, especially if they intend to take a lump-sum pension distribution.

Deciding how and where to invest your money can be daunting. First, identify your investment goals: income, growth or a combination. Then, pick investments that fit your ability to handle risk.

You can hand your portfolio over to a professional money manager who will pursue your investment goals for a fee. Be careful to confirm your manager's credentials. Is he or she fully licensed? Check track records and references.

10. How much can you rely on Social Security?

Social Security was never intended to provide all of one's retirement income. The earlier you retire, the lower your monthly Social Security benefits will be because your benefits will have to last that much longer. For example, if you retire at age 62, your benefits will be 20 percent lower than if you wait until age 65.

Ms. Lee is Manager Marketing Strategy/Development Employee Financial Planning at IDS Financial Services in Minneapolis, Minnesota.

Determining Readiness for Retirement: Using Super's Career Concerns Inventory as a Retirement Counseling Tool

by Sherry E. Sullivan, Ph.D.

Over the next several decades the size of the older U.S. population is expected to increase dramatically. For instance, in 1980 there were 25.5 million Americans age 65 and over. It's estimated that by the year 2000, there will be approximately 30.6 million Americans aged 65 and over (Atchley, 1985).

Although the number of Americans approaching retirement is increasing each year, career development researchers have provided few insights on how to prepare people for the retirement transition (Hall, 1986). For example, 75% of the American Society for Personnel Administration members surveyed indicated that their firm has early retirement options (Morrison & Jedrziewski, 1988).

Organizations with these options usually give their employees only 60–90 days in which to make their decision to accept or reject the early retirement offer (Mutschler, 1986). Although the time in which to make this major life decision is short, few organizations provide retirement planning programs and still fewer provide counseling on how to decide on when to retire. Thus while older employees are being given greater career options, they are not being provided with the counseling needed to make the most of the opportunities.

Pre-retirement counselors need a tool to help employees examine their readiness for retirement. Super's Career Concerns Inventory, (CCI), could be used to differentiate people who are ready for retirement from those who should remain in the work force. The CCI is based on Super's Theory of Career Stages and over 20 years of research.

The purpose of this article is: (1) to lay the foundation for the use of the CCI by reviewing Super's Theory of Career Stages, (2) to explain how the CCI can be used as a career counseling tool and (3) to discuss the benefits of using the CCI as part of a firm's retirement planning program.

Super's Theory of Career Stages

The major theme underlying Donald Super's Theory of Career Stages is that people implement their self-concept through vocational choices. These choices can be summed up in a series of career stages. Each stage is characterized by the developmental tasks and psychological issues that are most frequently encountered at certain ages.

Super has identified the four career stages of exploration, establishment, maintenance and disengagement. The exploration career stage typically extends from age 15 to 25. During this period, people engage in self-examination and consider their occupational alternatives. Individuals crystallize their occupational preferences, specify what particular job or jobs they are most committed to pursuing and implement plans to obtain their chosen job objective. The psychological issues faced in this period include the need to search for and discover one's own values, interests and purpose in life, and the need to develop a realistic self-assessment of one's abilities.

In the establishment career stage, people try to make a place for themselves in their chosen occupation. Security is their objective. In this stage, people face the psychological tasks of dealing with feelings of failure, deciding how professionally and organizationally committed they will be, and making commitments to a spouse about life style, family, values and child rearing. The establishment stage typically extends from age 25 to 45.

In the maintenance career state (from age 45 to 65) people attempt to hold on to their positions and keep up to date on the newest developments in their field. Dealing with the competitiveness and aggression of younger workers, learning to substitute wisdom-based experience for immediate technical skills, becoming primarily concerned with the organization's welfare rather than one's own career and dealing with feelings of loss as children leave home and parents die are all psycho-logical issues which must be dealt with in this stage.

In the disengagement stage, people tend to slow down, plan for retirement and even-tually retire to leisure activities. People in this stage need to find nonwork sources of life satisfaction. They need to come to terms with the choices they have made in their lives. People who retire from the work force need to maintain a sense of self-worth. This stage extends from 60 on (Super, Thompson & Lindeman, 1988).

The Career Concerns Inventory

The Career Concerns Inventory, (CCI), is a 60 item scale based on Super's theory. Items relate to the concerns of the explo-ration, establishment, maintenance and dis-engagement career stages.

When examining a group with the youngest member age 50, it can be assumed that anyone in the exploration or establish-ment stage has recycled to that stage and is not in that stage for the first time. Recycl-ing can occur when people face failure, crisis or change in their occupational or personal life. Thus, the CCI can be used to divide older employees into three groups: maintainers, disengagers and recyclers.

The CCI can be administered to a large group or to an individual. It takes approxi-mately 30 minutes to complete the survey. The CCI contains statements of career concerns—psychological issues and devel-opmental tasks related to each of the stages.

For example, statements related to the concerns of the maintenance stage include: "Maintaining the occupational position I have achieved" and "Keeping up with the knowledge, equipment and methods in my field." Statements related to the concerns of the disengagement stage include: "Cutting

down on my working hours," "Developing more hobbies to supplement work interest," and "Talking to retired friends about retire-ment and adjustment." Statements related to the concerns of the recycling stage, (i.e., combination of exploration and establish-ment stage questions) include: "Finding the work I am best suited for" and "Finding opportunities to do work I really enjoy." People indicate the degree to which each statement is of concern or of immediate importance to them.

After the survey has been completed it can be scored by hand or by computer. Hand scoring takes approximately 15 min-utes when following the directions and conversion tables supplied in Super's coun-seling manual. This method is most appro-priate when scoring is to be completed by workshop participants or for immediate individual counseling. Computer scoring is available through the Consulting Psycholo-gist Press. It is recommended for use with large groups or for needs analysis because statistical data on the group is provided (Super et al., 1988).

After the CCI has been scored, counsel-ing should be tailored to reflect the needs of individuals based on their career stage. For instance, people in the disengagement stage are probably ready for retirement. Their minds are occupied with planning to leave the work force and developing nonwork activities. Therefore, disengagers should be provided with retirement plan-ning such as information on financial planning, health, family relations and lei-sure activities.

In contrast, people in the maintenance stage are not ready to retire. They are con-cerned with maintaining their position in the work force and keeping up to date in their field. One of the major complaints of maintainers is that career counseling stopped once they were socialized into the organization (Hall, 1986).

Managers need to spend time and resources developing the talents of their midcareer employees just as they spend time and resources strengthening the confidence of newcomers. Re-training may be needed so that maintainers can avoid midcareer plateauing.

If people in the maintenance stage were offered an option to retire, it may not be in their best interests to do so. Retiring and leaving the work force would probably result in dissatisfaction and poor adjustment to retirement. If the maintainers accepted an early retirement buy-out option because the monetary rewards are too great to pass up, they should be counseled to seek employment with another organization or engage in volunteer work.

Finally, recyclers may be the most difficult employees to counsel as they are examining their lives much as they did when they were teen-agers. However unlike teen-agers, recyclers usually receive little or no counseling and must often re-establish their career path by themselves. People in the recycling stage are motivated by the need to re-evaluate their career choices and to change their occupational or work environment. They need information on second careers, educational opportunities and how to market their skills in order to avoid age discrimination.

Some books that may be especially helpful to recyclers include: *What Color is Your Parachute?* (Bolles, 1988), *Finding the Right Job at Midlife* (Allen & Gorkin, 1985) and *Success over Sixty* (Myers & Andersen, 1984). These books provide information from how to prepare a resume to self-analysis exercises that help people determine what skills they have and what skills they most enjoy

using. Also, recyclers may benefit from membership in organizations such as the Over 40 Club, which provides peer support for career changers.

In sum, the CCI can be a valuable career counseling tool because it provides information on the type of development program people need based on their career stage rather than on their age. Instead of forcing all people of a certain age to prepare for retirement, the CCI provides a means for distinguishing those who will benefit most from pre-retirement counseling (i.e., those who are ready for retirement), from those who would benefit from other types of career counseling.

Benefits of Using the CCI

There are three major benefits to be derived from the use of the CCI as part of a company's pre-retirement program. First the CCI can be used to differentiate employees who are ready for retirement from those who should remain in the work force. Being able to differentiate those older employees who wish to remain in the work force will be especially important in the years to come due to the anticipated decrease in the number of younger workers.

For example, by the year 1990 there will be 44% fewer people in the age 18–25 group than there were in 1980. The fast food industry is already experiencing a shortage of workers due to the decreasing number of teen-agers (Johnson, 1989). To combat this shrinking number of teen workers, organizations like McDonald's are targeting recruiting advertisements to retirees. As more organizations experience this shrinking of the labor force, they will also need to develop strategies to employ all available workers. McDonald's McMasters program, Disney

World's retiree work vouchers and Traveler's Corporation's re-employment program may be prototypes for the future wide-spread re-employment of retirees.

Second, the CCI can be used in conjunction with other surveys to get a more complete understanding of a person's career orientation. For instance, the Strong-Campbell Interest inventory should be used to determine a person' vocational interests and the Values Scale could be used to determine how important achievement, personal growth, security and economic rewards are to the person (Super et al., 1988). The CCI is a flexible tool that can be easily added to other information surveys an organization is already using.

Third, CCI adds the ingredient most pre-retirement programs lack—it provides information on when a person is ready to retire. Determining if a person is ready to retire should be the first step in any retirement preparation program. Time and money should not be wasted preparing someone for retirement who is really in need of skill training to avoid plateauing or information on preparing for a second career.

As we enter the 1990s and move from the baby boom to the baby bust, we must consider new ways in which to more fully utilize our aging work force. To realize the potential of our older workers, we must begin with a determination of which people are the most likely candidates for continued employment and which people are ready for retirement.

References

Allen, J. & Gorkin, L. (1985) *Finding the Right Job at Midlife.* New York: Simon & Schuster, Inc.

Atchley, R. (1985) *Social Forces and Aging.* Belmont: Wadsworth.

Bolles, R. (1989) *What Color is Your Parachute?* Berkeley: Ten Speed Press.

Hall, D. (1986) Breaking career routines: Midcareer choice and identity development. In Hall, D. (ed.) *Career development in organizations.* San Francisco: Jossey-Bass Publishers.

Johnson, H. (1988) Retirement: Older workers help meet employment needs. *Personnel.*

Morrison, M. & Jedrziewski, M. (1988) Retirement planning: Everybody Benefits. *Personnel Administrator.*

Mutschler, M. (1986) How golden a handshake? Reactions to early retirement incentive plans. *Compensation and Benefits Management.*

Myers, A. & Andersen, C. (1984) *Success Over Sixty.* New York: Summit Books.

Super, D. (1957) *Psychology of careers.* New York: Harper & Brothers.

Super, D., Thompson, A. & Lindeman, R. (1988) *Adult Career Concerns Inventory: Manual for Research and Exploratory Use in Counseling.* Palo Alto, CA: Consulting Psychologists Press, Inc.

The Career Concerns Inventory can be purchased from the Consulting Psychologists Press, 577 College Ave., Palo Alto, CA 94306.

Dr. Sullivan is a professor at Fogelman College of Business and Economics at Memphis State University, Memphis, Tennessee.

Is It Early Retirement or Age Discrimination?

by Christine Masters, J.D.

I went to work at the United States Equal Employment Opportunity Commission in 1978, the year that agency assumed responsibility for enforcing the federal statute against age discrimination in employment. Thus began my interest in gerontology and older workers.

In 1982, I joined the firm of Allred, Maroko, Goldberg & Ribakoff, continuing to handle an ever increasing number of claims of age discrimination. In 1989, my office here in Los Angeles received 235 requests for representation in age-related employment problems.

In line with my belief that prevention is the best remedy for age discrimination, I began a consulting practice, Innovative Solutions, to assist small to medium size employers in more effectively utilizing older workers.

I will focus on the preventative measures professionals need to be aware of in preparing and offering retirement packages.

Will a special early retirement package be deemed to be a form of coercion to get an older person who has not yet reached retirement age out of the work force, and thus be age discrimination? Are there any situations in which an employer is entitled to require persons to retire? Can an employer force an employee to choose between severance benefits and early retirement?

Laws Prohibiting Age Discrimination

Two statutory schemes, one state and one federal, prohibit discrimination on the basis of age in employment.

The Age Discrimination in Employment Act of 1967

Congress originally struggled over inclusion of a prohibition on age discrimination in the Civil Rights Act of 1964. No consensus was reached until the Age Discrimination in Employment Act of 1967 ("ADEA") was enacted three years later, originally to be enforced by the United States Department of Labor. Since 1978, the ADEA has been enforced by the United States Equal Employment Opportunity Commission.

The ADEA provides in pertinent part that: It is unlawful to fail or refuse to hire or to discharge any individual . . . because of such individual's age.

The ADEA applies to those employers with 20 or more employees and to those individuals over age 40.

The California Fair Employment and Housing Act

The California Fair Employment and Housing Act ("FEHA") has prohibited discrimination in employment for many years. It was amended in 1980 to prohibit specifically discrimination on account of age. The FEHA applies to those employers with five or more employees.

Both the state and federal laws are enforced by administrative agencies; both have time requirements within which a person must act; and both provide for civil action if there is no successful resolution administratively.

Discrimination

The word "discrimination" merely means to make a distinction. Discrimination is not necessarily unlawful. It only becomes unlawful where the distinction in on account of a prohibited basis, such as age. Providing unlawful discrimination is usually accomplished by one of two means.

Disparate Treatment

This theory is illustrated by examining the treatment of two similarly situated employees, both performing their jobs satisfactorily. The older one is terminated while the younger one is not. From that difference in treatment, the law allows us to draw a rebuttable presumption; in absence of the articulation of a legitimate, business-related, non-discriminatory reason, we can conclude that age was a motivating factor in the decision to terminate the older employee.

Of course, the employer is allowed to proffer evidence of a non-discriminatory motive, and unless the employee shows that the employer's articulate reason is non-believable or is a mere pretext for ageism, there will be no finding of unlawful discrimination.

In the example above, if the employer offers evidence that the older individual is terminated because of excessive absenteeism and that other younger individuals are terminated under the same circumstances, the employer has adduced sufficient evidence to rebut the presumption that age played a part in the termination decision, and no liability will be imposed.

Disparate Impact

An alternative theory of proving age discrimination allows examination of the treatment of a whole class of people affected by a facially neutral rule or action, e.g., job elimination during a merger. If one can show by statistical analysis that the apparently neutral act disproportionately affects a protected group, i.e., those over 50, again the law allows a rebuttable presumption that age was a factor in the selection of those to be eliminated. Proof of illicit motive or intent is irrelevant because impact analysis is designed to implement the congressional concern with the consequences of employment practices.

Remedies

Assuming discrimination is proven, both the federal and state laws provide substantial relief to an aggrieved individual.

1. Under the ADEA, one may recover:

   a. Back pay, i.e., what the individual would have earned but for the unlawful act, minus what he or she has in fact earned;

   b. Liquidated damages—a like amount to backpay "double damages" where violation is "willful";

   c. Attorneys' fees and costs; and

   d. Miscellaneous: "make whole" remedies, such as reinstatement or other job benefits.

2. Under the FEHA, one may recover:

   a. Back pay and benefits;

   b. Compensatory damages for emotional pain and suffering;

   c. Punitive damages;

   d. Attorneys' fees and costs; and

   e. Miscellaneous "make whole" remedies.

Damage awards may be substantial, particularly if discrimination is alleged by an older, often long term, highly paid employee with whom juries tend to empathize. In California an average verdict for age and/or wrongful termination cases of over $500,000 was noted in a recent survey, with a few multi-million dollar awards: $44.8 million against Hilton Hotels; $26 million against John Hancock Mutual Life Insurance; and $9 million against Xerox Corporation.

Early Retirement

It is becoming increasingly common in this time of corporate mergers and acquisitions for employers to eliminate employees as a cost savings measure, either with an offer of early retirement to induce employees to leave voluntarily in exchange for some enhanced benefits, or through a forced reduction. A 1989 Fortune 100 study by the U.S. General Accounting Office revealed almost 80% had offered an early retirement program at least once between 1979 and 1989.

Frequent litigation has resulted, resulting in many large verdicts, where the employer has not properly or thoroughly addressed the issues in defending an early retirement package as being voluntary.

Validity of Waivers

Many employers attempt to limit liability during a reduction in force by having employees sign waivers or releases of age claims and other legal claims in exchange for some consideration such as enhanced retirement benefits or severance pay. The problem is that waivers tend to be used in cases of unequal bargaining power, and courts have upheld waivers only where the employer can demonstrate that the employee knowingly and voluntarily waived his or her private rights.

In several decisions in the mid 1980's the courts were quite cautious in finding that an employee voluntarily and knowingly accepted an early retirement package. The concern was that the employees, fearful of termination if they didn't accept, were forced to give up employment, without a fair evaluation of their legal rights and remedies and perhaps without fair compensation. An older worker who is not fully cognizant of his/her rights under the ADEA and worried about making ends meet, might feel like there's no choice and sign.

Mandatory Retirement

Since 1986 when Congress amended the ADEA, mandatory retirement at any age has been strictly prohibited. An exception to this general rule under the ADEA is made for executives or high level policy makers, who may be retired as early as age 65, providing that they have been employed for the preceding two (2) years in a "bonafide executive or high policy making position" and are eligible to receive an immediate aggregate annual retirement benefit of at least $44,000. Congress felt that the exemption was necessary to assist employers in predicting retirement patterns, assuring promotions and changing top management to make room for young achievers.

The EEOC has issued administrative guidelines interpreting this exemption which is to be narrowly construed, and there have been several decisions interpreting "high-level executive".

Severance Pay versus Early Retirement

It is quite clear that employers may not deny severance pay to employees who are also eligible for retirement benefits in situations in which younger persons are given severance benefits. This means that if a company is going to engage in a reduction in force with enhanced severance benefits for those individuals who voluntarily separate from employment, they cannot refuse to pay older workers their vested retirement benefits in addition to the offered enhanced severance benefits. If employment is not going to be severed, but the employee is merely given an opportunity to accept some special layoff benefits or to volunteer to retire early, there is no ADEA violation.

Practical Advice

If you are involved in assisting an employer offering a retirement package, there are a few things that you can watch for or that you can tell the employer to watch for to avoid future legal claims.

Look at the impact on the older worker population within the company. Age audits of personnel should be a part of any decision to layoff or engage in job elimination either through enhanced severance benefits or early retirement packages. If the employer is seeking a release from those individuals who accept enhanced benefits, make sure the release is clear, unambiguous and highlighted. Make sure the employees have an opportunity to ask questions and understand what they are giving up if they choose to accept an early retirement.

Many companies have found that offering early retirement carries a huge initial cost, and that they lose employees that they can least afford to lose. Make sure that the early retirement incentives are not offered selectively. The same offer must be made to the entire company or corporate division. Finally, if the employer is utilizing salary as a factor in making its decision to lay off employees or offer benefits, make sure the same criteria are applied across the board.

Early retirement is a two-edged sword. While encouraging older workers to quit allows talented younger employees a chance to rise faster, some analysts believe early retirement incentive programs cause harm by weakening employee loyalty among workers of all ages.

Many companies have found that the early retirement packages were much more costly than anticipated given heavy pension and retiree health care costs. Given the high cost of litigation in the event that an employee is dissatisfied or feels forced out, employers would best be advised to embark upon these programs with extreme caution.

Ms. Masters is associated with the law firm of Allred, Maroko, Goldberg & Ribakoff, Los Angeles, California.

7

RETIREE RELATIONS

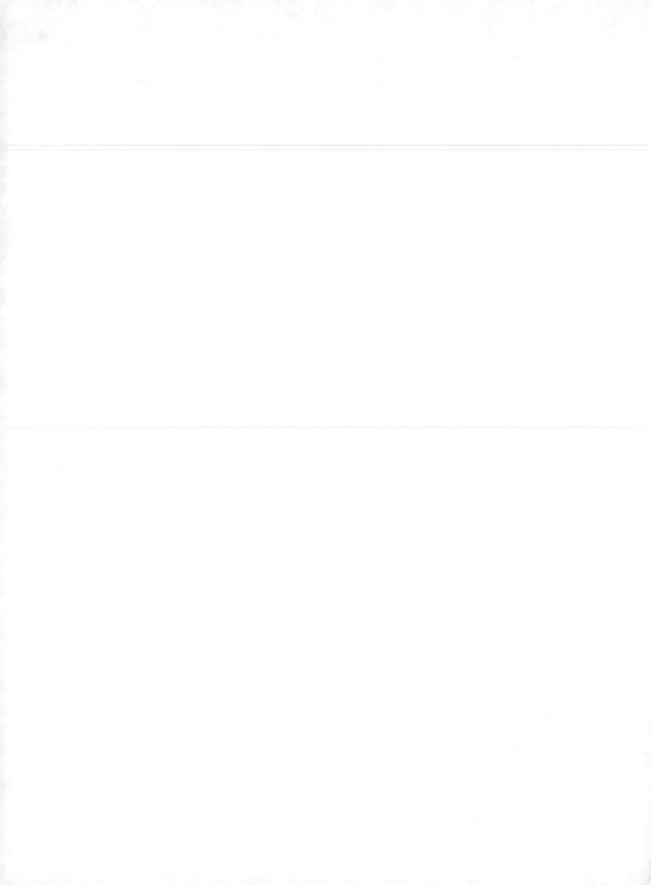

Retirement Planning: Everybody Benefits

ASPA-ISPP National Survey of Retirement Preparation Policies and Practices

by Malcolm H. Morrison and M. Kathryn Jedrziewski

Summary

During 1985–1986 the American Society for Personnel Administration Foundation (ASPA) provided grant funds to the International Society of Preretirement Planners (ISPP) to conduct a national survey of retirement preparation policies and practices in American business and industry. Through this survey ASPA and ISPP wanted to secure up-to-date information on retirement preparation policies and practices, to share this information with their members and the public and to identify the future directions of retirement planning in the United States. More than 32,000 members of ASPA served as the universe for this study, and the ASPA national headquarters coordinated the mailing and return of survey questionnaires. The survey had a high response rate and the results may thus be considered broadly representative of national corporate retirement policies and practices.

This survey covered major areas of retirement policies and practices, including:

- *early and very early retirement options;*

- *details of retirement preparation programs;*

- *post-retirement benefits;*

- *programs for older workers;*

- *future corporate needs for retirement planning information and programming.*

In general, respondents indicated a high degree of interest in retirement planning issues and retirement policies. While about 75 percent of firms had early retirement options, only 17 percent had implemented early retirement incentive programs (ERIPs). Nearly two-thirds of the firms provided retirement preparation information to their employees, but most did not do so through formal retirement preparation programs. There was wide interest in securing additional information about retirement preparation, with particular interest in program design and administration and key retirement issues: financial planning, health, legal issues and retirement adjustment. There is a growing national interest in providing employees with practical and effective information concerning retirement and in developing more creative approaches for communicating retirement planning information.

Employers are seeking to communicate better with both prospective and current retirees as pension and health benefit policies are changed.

The National Survey of Retirement Preparation Policies and Practices was designed to obtain clear information from employers about the current status of retirement planning programs and related policies. In addition, the survey was also intended to identify the major concerns of human resource and employee benefit professionals about state-of-the-art retirement preparation programs. Knowledge of these concerns should lead to improvements in retirement preparation programs.

With the continuation of early retirement and the expanding obligation of firms to provide post-retirement benefits including pensions, health and life insurance, and other benefits, providing information to pre- and post-retirees about their benefit options and retirement planning is an important area of corporate concern. The survey findings indicate progress is being made by employers in providing retirement planning information to employees and retirees. But, the results also demonstrate that despite the vast expansion of retirement information in recent years, most employers still do not have formal retirement preparation programs in place and many firms continue to seek very basic information about the design, content and administration of these programs.

These findings present a challenge to today's human resource professionals who are already experiencing the "retirement revolution." In the next 30 years, more employees will retire than at any other time in history. Thus, the need for innovative and dynamic retirement planning will grow significantly. The findings from the ASPA-ISPP survey provide a basis for developing creative retirement preparation programs and related policies. The survey findings clearly identify the needs of human resource professionals for up-to-date information on retirement preparation programs and document that improved communication with employees who will retire is an important continuing goal of organizations.

Characteristics of Companies Responding to Survey

Manufacturing firms represented the largest category of respondents—41 percent; finance, insurance and real estate organizations—14 percent; transportation and public

utilities—4 percent; state/local government—4 percent, and educational organizations—3 percent. Taken together, these organizations represented 66 percent of respondents. The remaining 34 percent were from a wide variety of organizational types (Figure 1).

Survey respondents were almost exclusively employed as human resources and personnel professionals in business firms. Nearly 75 percent were either managers/supervisors (42 percent) or directors/officers (30 percent) of the companies responding to the survey.

The average number of employees in responding firms was nearly 8,000, of whom an average, 45 percent, were salaried, and 55 percent hourly. Of hourly workers, 23 percent were represented by a union.

Early Retirement Policies

The average current age of retirement for all firms was 63; however, more than 70 percent of firms have an early retirement option for both salaried and hourly employees, connected with their primary pension plans. These options usually permit retirement as early as age 55 for salaried and hourly employees (Figure 2). Nearly 90 percent of the firms both provide information to employees about the provisions of their early retirement programs and believe that it is very important to communicate these provisions to employees well before they retire.

Over the past five years, many firms have implemented early retirement incentive programs (ERIP) in which employees who meet certain age and service requirements are permitted to accept very early retirement usually with compensation and/or pension bonus payments. The survey specifically inquired about firms' experience with such programs, especially regarding whether retirement preparation programs were provided to employees who accepted

Respondents to National Survey of Retirement Planning by Type of Industry			
Industry Type	Number Responding	Percent	Cumulative Percent
Manufacturing	223	41.0	41.0
Finance, insurance, real estate	75	13.9	54.9
Transportation and public utilities	23	4.2	59.1
State/local government	20	3.7	62.8
Education	17	3.1	65.9
Retail trade	14	2.6	68.5
General services	13	2.4	70.9
Wholesale trade	12	2.2	73.1
Communications	12	2.2	75.3
Mining	8	1.5	76.8
Construction	7	1.3	78.1
Research and development	5	.9	79.0
Federal government	3	.6	79.6
Agriculture	3	.6	80.2
Other (miscellaneous)	109	20.2	100.4
Total:	544	100.4	100.4

Figure 1

Earliest Age of Retirement Permitted in Company Pension Plans for Salaried and Hourly Employees		
Age	Percent of Pension Plans Permitting Retirement (Salaried Employees)	Percent of Pension Plans Permitting Retirement (Hourly Employees)
50	4.8	4.5
55	69.8	65.5
60	7.3	10.3
62	5.4	6.8
65	4.8	5.0
Other/not specified	7.7	8.5

Figure 2

very early retirement options. First, it was discovered that only about 17 percent of surveyed firms had ever used such ERIP programs at any time and that there was a tendency to offer such programs to salaried employees. Second, the great majority of firms provided information on the provisions of these programs to employees and believed that this type of communication was extremely important. (Spouses, however, received this type of information far less frequently—only about one third of the time.) Third, the results indicated that retirement preparation "programs" were offered to employees who accepted the very early retirement options. Overall, retirement preparation was offered to 55 percent of employees; the programs that were provided consisted of the firm's regular retirement preparation program (specially designed programs were used only about one-third of the time); and in the large majority of cases (75 percent), the retirement preparation provided did not include training for planning a second career. This is clearly an area where organizations should focus if they have early retirement incentive programs. Other research (Mutschler, 1986) has in fact indicated that in light of the short periods during which early retirement incentive program decisions must be made (often 60–90 days), more counseling about post-retirement employment would be desirable and might lead to more people working after retirement.

The results of the survey show clearly that both regular early retirement options and early retirement incentive programs continue to be offered by business firms and that information on these options is provided to employees. But, despite these efforts, the information reaching employees and their spouses may not be complete and in many instances, consideration of post-retirement employment options is not being adequately addressed by employer communication packages and programs.

Post-Retirement Benefits and Employment Options

There has been considerable national discussion about corporate benefits provided for retirees and the extent to which firms are providing employment opportunities for older workers. Survey results indicate activity in both of these areas of concern.

Companies are providing a variety of employee benefits for retired workers. The data indicate that 80 percent of firms are providing health insurance and 60 percent provide life insurance for retirees. Nearly half the firms have a retiree newsletter and about 20 percent provide retiree clubs, special activities and/or discounts. Yet, only 4 percent had programs to employ their own annuitants. (Pre-retirement educational assistance is provided by nearly 30 percent of firms.)

While firms do not usually have formal programs to hire annuitants, many do provide opportunities for older workers, some of whom may be their own retirees. More than 40 percent provide for part-time employment or consulting work after retirement and 25 percent have opportunities for seasonal or part-year work after retirement. Only a small number of firms provide gradual retirement or job-sharing programs for retiring employees.

Earlier retirement therefore has been accompanied by a significant broadening of employee benefits for retired workers and by opportunities for post-retirement employment. However, despite the existence of these opportunities, national data continue to indicate that relatively few retired employees continue to work. The continuing aging of the population, coupled with demand for workers may gradually bring about an increase in "retired workers" as we approach and pass the year 2000 (Morrison, 1986).

Retirement Preparation Programs

Despite the widespread interest in retirement policies, employee benefits for the retired and recognition of the need to communicate provisions of corporate retirement programs, many firms continue to have only limited familiarity with formal retirement preparation programs. The survey in fact indicated that while only 3 percent of organizations had never heard about such programs, 32 percent had never examined them and only 11 percent had detailed familiarity with such programs. Altogether, about 40 percent of firms reported that they had become familiar with, administered or conducted such programs. These findings imply that many firms still do not have formal retirement preparation programs in place and perhaps more important, existing programs may not be designed to communicate the specific provisions of the employee benefit programs of individual firms.

Because a significant percentage of firms do not yet use formal retirement preparation programs, the survey inquired about the pros and cons of these programs for the point of view of responding firms. These responses provide insight into why some firms have adopted programs and others have not.

The most important reasons favoring retirement preparation programs were:

- helping employees to be better prepared for retirement

- providing important planning information to employees

- assisting employees with decision-making

- improving employee well being and increasing productivity

The most important reasons against providing such programs were:

- programs are considered too costly

- programs are too time consuming to administer

- personnel are not available or qualified to conduct programs

- employees are not interested or have not requested such programs

There are significant differences between these clusters of answers. On one hand, it appears that firms view retirement preparation programs as highly beneficial for employees both before and after they retire. On the other, firms indicate that there are many administrative reasons why programs are not adopted and that these rationales may be independent of the value of such programs for employees. This may indicate that certain corporate cultures favor retirement preparation programs while others do not. At a minimum the findings indicate that a favorable view of retirement preparation programs is usually based on their value to employees, whereas an unfavorable view is based primarily on perceived administrative burdens.

In reviewing the ways in which firms provide retirement preparation information to employees, some important findings emerged. Almost two-thirds of the firms provide such information to retiring employees but only 35 percent of these do so using formal retirement preparation programs involving seminars, individual counseling and financial counseling. The majority (56 percent) provide some information to employees on a limited number of topics, such as pension benefits and health insurance. By a substantial margin (65 percent), most retirement preparation information and formal programs are developed by company personnel. Only in 18 percent of the cases were programs purchased from national or local vendors. Similarly, in most cases (65 percent), retirement preparation information and programs are provided to employees completely by company personnel.

The survey also revealed that three main techniques are used to communicate retirement preparation information:

- individual counseling

- group discussions

- invited experts on retirement topics

Individual counseling is clearly the most popular approach (71 percent) with group discussions (51 percent) and invited experts (46 percent) somewhat less significant. Despite its perceived popularity, individual financial counseling was used by only 13 percent of the firms although group sessions on personal financial planning were often used. About half the firms reported involving spouses in their programs and about one quarter also had post-retirement contact with retirees. Nearly two thirds of retirement programs and/or information are offered during regular working hours and at all corporate locations. Programs and information are usually provided to all employees, both salaried and hourly.

Personnel administrators and employee benefit specialists have consistently indicated interest in the content and timing of retirement preparation programs and/or information sessions. The survey provided valuable information about these concerns.

With regard to the major areas of retirement preparation information presented in most programs or information sessions, organizations clearly concentrate their efforts on: pension plans; Social Security and Medicare; personal financial planning;

estate planning; adjustment to retirement; investments; health prevention; and legal concerns. Other areas including employment, housing, long term care, family relationships, education, etc., receive less attention (Figure 3). Notably, certain issues that have received wide public attention, including long-term care, family relationships and sexuality, were infrequently included in corporate programs.

In terms of timing, about 15 percent of programs/information sessions are provided as early as age 50; about 26 percent by age 55 and about 6 percent by age 60. About half the programs do not have a specified age for participation. However, it is well known that most organizations do not encourage employees to participate in retirement preparation prior to age 50.

Since the survey indicated that two thirds of the firms now provide retirement preparation information or programs and many other firms have considered adding retirement preparation to their human resource program, examining the types of retirement preparation information that firms report would be most useful is of significance to human resource administrators and retirement planning professionals. The most important areas where additional information is needed are: designing retirement preparation programs; adjustment to retirement; administering programs; personal financial planning; Social Security/Medicare and legal concerns. Also important were post-retirement counseling; estate planning; national retirement policy and local community resources for retirees. Again, some areas that have received considerable national interests, such as second careers, volunteering, family relationships and long-term care, were mentioned much less frequently in terms of needed information (Figure 4).

Types of Retirement Preparation Information Presented by Firms

Type of Information	Percentage of Firms Presenting
Company pension plans	93.6
Social Security/Medicare	78.4
Corporate health insurance	60.2
Adjustment to retirement	48.0
Personal financial planning	42.4
Estate planning	36.3
Health prevention	32.5
Legal concerns	32.5
Investments	31.3
Volunteering	28.1
Part-time employment	25.7
Second careers	25.7
Psychological problems	23.1
Educational opportunities	22.5
Housing options	22.2
Widows/widowers	21.3
Relocation	20.2

Figure 3

Conclusion

Retirement preparation programming is growing in U.S. business firms. This is partly due to the continuation of early and very early retirement options provided through employee benefit plans. An additional impetus for communicating retirement planning information is the rising cost of employee benefits (particularly health insurance) for retirees. Formal retirement preparation programs are still not offered by the majority of firms but most do provide retirement planning information to employees. The information that is provided is still generally limited to financial, health insurance and legal concerns, although the areas of personal financial planning and adjustment to retirement are receiving increased attention. Areas of growing concern to professional retirement planners and specialists in aging, such as post-retirement employment, educational opportunities, health prevention and long-term care, are still not receiving significant attention in retirement preparation programming.

Firms are particularly interested in improved program designs and methods of program administration, further detailed information on Social Security/Medicare provisions and personal financial planning techniques. Thus, so far as firms are concerned, there remains a significant need for more comprehensive retirement preparation information and more effective program design and administration. Retirement

Retirement Preparation Information Needs of Firms

Type of Information	Percentage of Firms Suggesting Needs
Designing programs	37.2
Adjustment to retirement	35.3
Program administration	32.6
Personal financial planning	32.2
Social Security/Medicare	26.0
Legal concerns	25.1
Postretirement counseling	23.1
Estate planning	22.0
National retirement policy	21.3
Local resources	19.5
Medi-gap health insurance	18.9
Flexible employee benefit plans	18.2
Second careers	16.9
Preventive health care	16.8
Part-time employment	16.6
Vendor programs	16.0
Volunteering	15.1
Family relationships	11.1
Long-term care	7.8

Figure 4

planning and human resource professionals should begin to focus on these needs as we approach the aging and retirement of the baby boom population.

References

Morrison, M.H. "Work and Retirement in an Older Society," in *Our Aging Society, Paradox and Promise*, Pifer, A., and Bronte, L., (eds.), W.W. Norton & Company, New York: 1986.

Morrison, M.H. *The Transition to Retirement: The Employer's Perspective*, Bureau of Social Science Research, Inc., Washington, D.C., 1985.

Morrison, M.H. "Retirement and Human Resource Planning for the Aging Workforce," *Personnel Administrator*, June, 1984.

Morrison, M.H. "Corporate Practices: Personnel Programs and Management Strategies for Older Workers," *America's Aging Workforce*, Travelers Insurance Companies, 1986.

Mutschler, P.H. "How Golden a Handshake? Reactions to Early Retirement Incentive Plans," *Compensation and Benefits Management*, Summer, 1986.

Administration, 606 North Washington Street, Alexandria, Virginia 22314.

Malcolm H. Morrison is president of A.C.T. II Employee Benefit and Retirement

Planning, an employee benefit communica-tion firm in Columbia, Maryland.

M. Kathryn Jedrziewski is research coor-dinator at the Research and Training Center for Rehabilitation of Elderly Disabled Indi-viduals, School of Medicine, University of Pennsylvania.

Survey of ISRP Members on Non-Financial Retirement Benefits

by Alan J. Fredian, Ph.D. and Paul B. Grant

"Our health insurance department fills out Medicare claim forms for our retirees," one respondent commented. Another said "Retirees get the same dis-count on purchasing company products as our officers and employees."

These are a few of the written comments included in a survey of the members of the International Society for Retirement Plan-ning. The survey, conducted in 1989, was designed to learn more about some of the low cost benefits organizations are provid-ing their retirees.

The survey questionnaire was sent to nearly 500 organizations including busi-nesses, health care institutions and uni-versities. Over 100 surveys were returned and 82 were tabulated. The others were returned either partly filled out or entirely blank with a description of a company pro-gram attached to it.

Employment Opportunities for Retirees

One of the most striking findings is that 84.1 percent of the respondents indicated that they offer opportunities for retirees to remain active in the organization. The employment relationship and percent of respondents offering it follows:

Employment	Percent
Hired as consultant	70.7
Hired as temporary	63.4
Hired for special projects	59.8
Reemployed part time	58.5
Reemployed full time	31.7
Used as guest speaker	30.5
Served on Board	14.6
Retrained for new position	13.4
Mentored new employees	8.5
Used to orient new employees	7.3
Served as company tour guide	7.3

There is undoubtedly some overlap in the first four categories. A distinction should be made between the nature of the employment situation and the activities the retiree engages in. In addition to paid employment, 23.2% of the respondents invite the retirees back to perform voluntary activities.

Communication

While work is an important activity for both the retiree and the organization, many employers believe it is important to continue communicating with their retirees. Some of the motives are economic, i.e., presumably retirees are more likely to be ready to work and will be more productive if they are kept informed about what's going on in the company. Others feel it is good public and employee relations to communicate with retirees on a regular basis. The forms which the communication take vary.

Retiree Associations and Clubs. Twenty-nine point three percent sponsor a retiree association or club. Two thirds of the associations were started by the employer and nearly 60% provide some kind of space for the club. The space most often is a conference room or the cafeteria for meetings. Once in a while there may be desk space in the benefits office.

Almost all (71%) of the organizations sponsoring clubs provide some form of support. This assistance usually means clerical help, a staff coordinator, publicity and help with mailing, including printing and postage.

Thirty-three percent of the respondents, whether they have a club or not, employ a staff person to coordinate retirees' activities. The title of the person includes Retirement Services Administrator and Manager of Pension Relations as well as an assortment of generic titles from the benefits and human resources area.

The activities of the club are administered by the employer, the retiree association itself or some combination of the two. The latter is the most common.

The activities engaged in vary. Some of the most commonly mentioned activities include educational programs about the company and its products, social activities, travel, newsletters, exercise and nutrition classes, social support networks, trips to sporting and cultural events, volunteering and bingo.

Beyond the usual activities described here, some report that the club is used to express retirees' concerns to management and also to lobby politically for the firm's and retirees' interests.

Other Communications. Some organizations use means other than the retiree association or club as a way to communicate with retirees. Sixty-eight percent send retirees the company newsletter. Others will send birthday cards (7.3%) and holiday greetings (16%). Twenty-two and a half percent use personal calls or interviews to explain changes in company goals or plans as well as changes in benefits.

Influencing the Community

Many of the respondents indicate that their organization tries to influence the community for the benefit of their retirees. This is how the respondents reported their community involvement:

Community Program	Percent
Health Fairs	65.0
Related education	50.0
Charity drives	45.0
Counseling	30.0
Referral Services	25.0

Other Reasons for Inviting Retirees Back

Almost 70% of the organizations invite retirees back on a regular basis, most often for some kind of recreation or celebration—service award dinners, Christmas or holiday parties, picnics, golf outings, etc. Apart from regularly scheduled events, nearly half of the companies bring retirees back for new product announcements, changes in ownership, etc.

The Future

Some of the respondents (12.2%) plan on implementing new benefits within the next 12 months. Typically the new benefit involves educational or social activities such as post retirement counseling and planning, health and fitness planning and activities, starting a retiree association, newsletter, and/or membership in AARP or other retiree associations.

Many of the survey participants took time to write comments. Most believe that their organizations derive a good return for their modest investment in these non-financial post retirement benefits.

Many infer that they are pleased to have an able and experienced work force available to their employer. Others believe that those retirees who participate in their program are psychologically and physically more healthy and the results will eventually be demonstrated in reduced retiree health care costs.

This conclusion may be premature. It is also possible that those retirees who are healthy are more likely to become involved than those who are not. Nevertheless, there is considerable optimism and enthusiasm voiced by the survey participants. Most of those surveyed would probably agree with one respondent who wrote, "More needs to be done."

The authors are professors in Loyola University's Institute of Industrial Relations. Both serve on the university's Retirement Allowance Committee, which is concerned with pension and investment issues.

Insurer Overcomes Tax and Legal Complications to Create a Pool of Experienced Temporary Independent Contract Staffers

by Janet Lareau

Kemper National Insurance Companies, a property casualty insurance company, has been in the process of developing a retiree temporary work pool over the past two years.

The impetus came from our loss control, claim and underwriting departments which were in need of servicing accounts during heavy work load periods. They were looking for very specialized, trained personnel on a part-time basis to fill an immediate temporary need or to fill in until a permanent employee could be found. Retirees seemed to be the answer to the need.

The procedures to implement this pool posed some difficult questions. Persons hired as independent contractors can run into tax problems if they derive all their income from only one client. Also, they must go through the process of setting themselves up as independent contractors and obtain the necessary insurance coverage. There can also be tax consequences for the company if the IRS determines that an independent contractor is in fact an employee. The employer can be held liable for both the employee and employer portions of employment and income taxes and a 100% excise tax based on the amount of the tax liability.

One deterrent to Kemper hiring a retiree as a part-time employee was the stipulation in our retirement plan that employees cannot receive pension benefits while employed unless they come under the required distribution rules (having attained age 70 and one half).

It was felt that the retiree would not want to give up a pension benefit for a temporary part-time job. This has been solved by an amendment to our plan which allows Kemper retirees to be employed on a temporary basis as long as they work 200 hours or less in a 90 day period. Our legal advisor also had concerns about how Medicare would be handled for these temporary employees. Most of them are covered by the Kemper retiree health plan which becomes a supplement to Medicare at age 65.

Would Medicare deem that Kemper should be primary carrier for their health coverage which would then make Medicare the secondary payor? We contacted the Social Security Administration and asked just that question. The reply was that we must treat these employees the same as any other employees in the same situation. If health benefits are provided to part time/temporary employees, then health benefits would have to be provided to retiree temporaries.

Questions regarding age discrimination have also been addressed since retirees are in the protected age group. We cannot exclude older workers from participation in our benefit programs if younger workers in the same situation are allowed to participate. However, if there were a group of employees that were not offered health benefits and the retiree temporaries were included in that group, then the retiree temp would not have to be offered health benefits. (I must emphasize that we are not trying to deny benefits to the retirees, but the thinking is that they will retain their retiree benefits and retiree status.)

There is also the problem of nondiscrimination under the minimum coverage test of IRC 410(b), which provides that plans must benefit at least 70% of all nonhighly compensated employees. This test impacts both our defined benefit and defined contribution plans.

Part of the difficulty that we have faced in setting up the pool is, that in the past, Kemper has provided benefits to both temporary and part-time employees. Also, our method of crediting service has been by elapsed time, not credited hours.

For example, if an employee was hired on June 1, 1990, and is listed in our records as an active employee on June 1, 1991, that employee will have completed one year of service, regardless of the actual number of hours worked.

Even in the face of these difficulties, it was felt that there was enough merit in this idea that it was decided to investigate the subject further with the idea of expanding the plan and offering it to all retirees. This will give retirees a way to use their talents, earn some additional income, but have more control over and flexibility in their working hours.

An announcement will be sent to all retirees explaining the program with a questionnaire to be returned if the retiree is interested in being listed in the pool.

They will be asked to list their skills, what type of job might interest them and the locations where they would be available to work. Since our retirees move about a great deal, we might have a retiree who worked in Illinois, but is now living in Florida and would be available for work in our Orlando office.

It will also be explained that a retiree listed as being available to work as a temp does not guarantee a job offering.

During the time that we have been researching the feasibility of implementing a retiree temporary pool, the company has determined that our demand for all temporary workers will be better served if the company had its own pool of temporary workers, rather than hiring them from outside agencies.

Having researched the retiree question has made the implementation of the non-retiree pool a little easier. Our solution will be to set up a temporary pool which will include both retiree and non-retiree workers. There will be virtually no distinctions in the description of the characteristics for the two groups, and a uniform set of rules will apply to all pool participants.

The characteristics for the group will be: (1) Ability to turn down an assignment when offered; (2) Right to discontinue an assignment and go back into the pool with reasonable notice to the company; and (3) Be compensated on an hourly basis.

Specific requirements for the retiree members of the pool will be that there must be at least a 90 day "break in service" between the last day of regular employment and the first day that the retiree can apply to join the temporary pool.

This will enable the retiree to begin drawing retirement benefits. The retiree cannot work more than 200 hours in a quarter or distributions from the retirement plan will cease.

During two recent years, we have had a number of retirees work temporarily on a "by request" basis. We are looking forward to implementing the full program and using the many talents of our retirees.

There have been many questions posed and answered, but we feel that the resulting program will be worthwhile to both our retirees and the company.

Ms. Lareau is Corporate Benefits Coordinator for Kemper National Insurance Companies.

8

LOOKING TO THE FUTURE

Designing Tomorrow, Today—A Look at Challenges Facing Retirement Planners, by Ernest J. Savoie

Designing Tomorrow, Today—A Look at Challenges Facing Retirement Planners

by Ernest J. Savoie

We've all heard of Workforce 2000. Many of the same forces shaping the workforce of the next decade are also shaping what retirement will look like as we head into the next century—less than ten years away! It's always risky to predict the future. Even the best futurists frequently predict trends and events that never happen, or they overlook major developments that, in retrospect, might have been foretold.

Still, looking down the road—and maybe looking around the corner a little—can be a useful exercise. It can help us think ahead and help us design our individual and societal futures. Furthermore, it's always intriguing.

America's Changing Age Structure

A few demographic facts make a logical starting point. For openers, the size of the baby boom (1946–1964) and of the baby bust that followed (1964–present) will influence what life will be like in the next century.

The number of Americans 35–50 years old will grow four times as fast as those in any other age group. Also, by the year 2000, there will be 35 million people over 65. Now there are only 20 million. People over 65 will represent more than 17% of our population by 2020, versus 12% today. There's no changing these facts. And these facts will have a powerful impact on our society.

Some medical authorities predict the average life span might reach over 100 years in the future. Back in 1900 the life expectancy was 47.3 years. Today it's up to 74.7 years.

As a result, not far into the next century, for the first time in our history, American elders will outnumber American teens.

The United States is no longer the young nation that it was during its first 200-plus years. "Agequake" is about to shape America as much as the youth culture shook it in the 1960s.

Development Theory

These demographic facts are some of the reasons that many of our human development theories are being re-thought. Instead of sequential life stages, where we go from youth to middle to old age, Americans will experience "fluid" life cycles. Life stages will be intertwined and blended. And we'll no longer be able to assume that because people of one generation experienced life in a certain way, their children will duplicate that experience.

In the year 2000, most older people will be "improvising" their roles in life. There will be no "preconceived pattern" that most elders will be expected to follow. The impact will be not only on elders, but on all other groups as they inter-relate and provide goods and services to fast-living elders. An important focus of the impact will include housing, family, health, education and work—to name only a few obvious areas.

Housing

A rejuvenation of communal living is quite possible. Baby boomers in their older years may find this arrangement best meets their needs. But it will be a new form of communal living—not a room for Grandma or Grandpa back on the farm. Congregate or group living facilities—those offering shared shelter, services, and amenities—will grow. Zoning and housing laws will change to allow for renovation of single homes to multiple units.

Throughout the country, new insurance policies will be formulated to cover personal and property relationships between and among extended family and non-family members. There will be a growth in "house matching" services, combining social workers and housing experts to serve the new clientele.

Many elders will choose housing on the outskirts of college towns in order to be close to cultural activities and experiences.

Other people will go to Mexico or other overseas communities which will offer tax and cost incentives to get the spending power of retiree money.

And the Sunbelt will be bulging. Senator Daniel P. Moynihan claims that by the year 2020 it will take 44 lanes of highway to carry the traffic from Miami to Ft. Lauderdale. This will lead to other changes. Besides traffic congestion, limited water supplies will force people to look at different sections of the country. The northeast may be a potential retirement haven.

Family Relationships

Gerontologists predict that the majority of "older families" will be headed by women. Women already outlive men and make up the majority of the aged population.

The family make-up will be more complex. The notion of "family," which has been changing in recent generations, will continue to be altered by the elder baby boomers.

Many families will have been restructured by divorces and remarriages.

As a result, there will be "blended" and extended families. Also, a large number of independent older women who live alone will join with others to form new kinds of families of unrelated people. Blended and nontraditional family relationships will complicate notions of economic equity and what is the right and fair thing to do for children of different partners and different relationships.

The potential length of many marriages will be greater than ever. People will have to live together not just 10 years after retirement, but maybe 30 years. Many new adjustments will be required. There may be a lot more divorces and remarriages after 65. And when adjustments are successful, couples will divide up responsibilities in a more even split than we typically see now.

In the early twenty-first century, elders and children are likely to have a more complicated economic relationship. Many elders may very well find they have to give their adult children a helping hand. Parents who succeed in the boom years may feel resentful that their children didn't turn out "better." And children will feel let down if they are the first American generation to have a standard of living lower than their predecessors. At the same time, elders may have older parents to care for to an extent that generations before never had to.

The Impact of the "New Family" on Communities and Retirement Planning

Community projects may thrive as the new family unit works with others to address "issues of the day." In a more "open" society, lesbian and gay relationships could emerge as an acceptable lifestyle for many elders.

There will be a growing field of training and education in family development and family gerontology. Some shopping malls will incorporate community centers, offering a wide range of educational and personal improvement courses.

"Learn-at-home" will increase—via satellite, phone and computers. Schools-on-wheels may join meals-on-wheels.

We'll see a surge in "family therapists," and the rise of new services, such as businesses specializing in family reunion arrangements. Care giver and companionship services to the frail elderly will expand. Perhaps elders without children will "adopt" non-related couples and children as heirs, in return for companionship provided by the adopted family.

There will be new branches of family law and changes in estate planning to address unusual and complicated beneficiaries and heirs.

Governments, collective bargaining arrangements, businesses and organizations of all types will be pressured to revise laws, equities and benefits for our 35 million citizens over 65.

All these developments will have a major impact on retirement planning programs, on what they cover, on who gets them, and on who gives them. With people possibly living 30 years beyond official retirement, post-retirement planning may come into its own. Both pre-retirement and post-retirement programs will need to include a growing emphasis on women, on issues about outliving your family, and on developing "new" family units and relationships.

Medical and Health Care Implications

Medical researchers predict that within the next 10 years there will be protective vaccines for some kinds of cancers, artificial bones and blood and implanted pumps to deliver drugs automatically for conditions like diabetes. Along with new cures and new procedures, there will be an increased insight into the aging process itself. Drugs and treatments will be designed to deal with underlying physical and mental changes that produce the diseases that make us "age."

Brain research is one of the new frontiers of medical inquiry. The annual physical exam will probably include tests of short- and long-term memory as well as a "brain check." Geriatrics will attract more doctors—and more research money. Awareness programs for health practitioners on "ageism" will be required study.

On an institutional basis, medical centers of the future will be "networks." They'll serve as a hub of a group of hospitals, institutions, clinics and hospices. Hospitals will be reserved for tracking and for treatment of the most serious illnesses—those which require complex and expensive technology.

There will be an upsurge in home health care. House calls will come back—especially to the congregate living facilities. The doctor's "black bag" most likely will contain a portable computer linked to a data base system that tracks the patient's health condition and history.

Doctors and medical practitioners will have to know a lot more about the people end of the business. The relationship between health care practitioners will change. Nurses will make more money due principally to a tremendous shortage of nursing professionals. Pharmacists will play a more crucial role, and they will increasingly serve more as "health educators."

Self-help health groups will be on the rise. Holistic medicine also could come into its own. Nontraditional healing methods will be more widely accepted. Herbs and exotic potions may be more widely marketed.

The growing concern to protect the environment could affect the practice of medicine. About 25% of all prescription drugs are now derived from plants. For anti-cancer drugs, this figure approaches 40%. For the future, then, environmentalism could be a matter of life and death.

These medical developments will, of course, bring some social implications. The cost of health care and how health care is organized will be important public and private issues. Growing debates will take place on the ethics of who should have access to information, such as genetic profiles. "Right-to-die" issues and living wills will be commonly discussed among families and with doctors and lawyers.

Education and Work

In 1970, Richard Bolles coined the phrase "The Three Boxes of Life" in his book "What Color is Your Parachute?" The "boxes" are the worlds of education, work, and leisure.

Within the last couple of decades the boundaries of these "boxes," or life phases, have begun to blur. In the 21st century, multiple careers and employee retraining will blur them even more. The rigid concept of an employment cycle (i.e., retiring at 62 or 65) will no longer hold. The very word "career" may lose its current meaning.

Workers can expect multiple employment experiences after age 45—a time when we are supposed to have "settled down." Thus, there will be an explosive growth for retraining programs.

The labor pool is shrinking—it will be at an all-time low in the early 21st century. There will be shortages of young people who can do the jobs that need to be done. At the same time, there will be a larger pool of elders who are experienced, talented

and available. This will result in changes to current hiring practices and rigid job requirements.

There will be a growth in part-time work and in job-sharing. Fringe benefits will be developed to accommodate these new job arrangements. Workers will be offered more cafeteria-style benefits. Labor contracts will undergo changes to accommodate varied schedules and working conditions. "Earnings" penalties in lost Social Security benefits will be lessened. Non-monetary benefits, for example tuition subsidies, will increase. Eldercare and childcare leaves will be common. Women will play a significant role in "equalizing" pensions and other benefits.

Ken Dychtwald, in his book *Age Wave*, predicts that some workers may never retire. Or they may retire several times. He suggests that this may cause an intergenerational struggle: "age wars that will boil to the surface as older workers refuse to make room for the young ..."

The notion of "early retirement" probably won't exist in its current form in the future. Changing economic facts will create incentives for many to continue to work. Pensions will be worth less than they are today and fewer pensions will be guaranteed. Widespread bankruptcies may make it difficult, or impossible, for the government to guarantee pensions under ERISA or to guarantee IRAs.

In the year 2030 there will be 50 Social Security beneficiaries for every 100 covered workers. In 1991 there were slightly more than 30 beneficiaries to every 100 covered workers. Because of pressures on Social Security and on the economy, the government will try to increase the retirement age by various means. For many of our elder people, therefore, Retirement 2000 will not be retirement at all. It will be work, and part-time work.

All this suggests the future will see new variations of retirement. Entrepreneurship will thrive. Other retirees will re-enter the work force through retraining. (It's happening now; e.g., McDonald's has instituted a "McMaster" training program for elders.)

Still others will be extensively involved in volunteer work, home care or projects involving the environment. Mentoring will come of age. Women will play active roles as mentors of young women and girls. Forms of part-time employment, job sharing and phased retirement will become the preferred approach to easing into retirement. New programs and services will be needed for these "at-work" retirees.

Planning Implications

Financial, benefit and retirement planners will need to acquaint themselves with both monetary and nonmonetary benefits. There most likely will be extraordinary changes in pensions, health care and Social Security. Financial planning will take on new dimensions and more importance.

Retirement planning will become a new ballgame. With life phases being muted and a combination of work, education, and leisure throughout life becoming the norm, retirement planning probably will be renamed. The term "life planning" may take its place.

A core contribution that planners can make will be to shape retirement and life planning programs to instill a greater consciousness about what one can do for oneself. This self-help emphasis is necessary since society's resources will be less and the demands on the resources more.

Perhaps more significant is that this stress on self-empowerment is exactly what is needed to maximize individual health and self-worth.

For retirement professionals, Retirement 2000 is Opportunity 2000. As the supply of services races to catch up to the demand, innovation will be the order of the day. For all the reasons we have seen, the best planners will emphasize and promote the vision of The Elder Giver. This is the right individual and societal focus as planners help design the retirements of tomorrow.

Mr. Savoie is Director Employee Development for Ford Motor Company in Dearborn, Michigan.

9

PROFESSIONAL RESOURCES

- Personal Computer (PC) Software for Retirement Planners
- Books for Retirement Planners

Personal Computer (PC) Software for Retirement Planners

MERIT for Managing the Future

An interactive benefit communications and financial planning software program, providing employees with a proactive guidance system to help achieve and maintain financial security in retirement.

The Merit program is customized by entering a client company's full range of benefits, including qualified plan funding formulas and Section 125 options.

The employee, working at an IBM PC or compatible computer, uses 21 data entry screens to enter personal financial information. The employee sets goals and chooses MERIT—which stands for mortality-expenditures-rate of return-inflation-taxes—strategy assumptions.

The software (1) quantifies the dollars the employee must save and invest per month to achieve financial security; (2) provides a system for organizing and maintaining financial records; (3) projects federal income taxes; (4) compares Section 125 options to after-tax expenditures; (5) calculates the employee's actual pre-tax and after-tax rate of return on invested funds; and (6) provides the employee with flexibility in selection of retirement planning strategies.

From a sponsoring firm's viewpoint, the program can help control costs of escalating benefits, and helps employees understand the value of their total compensation and benefit package.

Produced by: MERIT Software Concepts, Kenneth L. Decker, President; P.O. Box 771966, Houston, TX 77215.

FRED: The Friendly Retirement Education Database

A computer software program to help employees deal on an individualized basis with personal issues such as finances, investments, budgeting, estate planning, family records, leisure time and lifestyle.

FRED is being marketed to profit and non-profit organizations for use by individual employees. It has the employee interact with a computer on personal issues, rather than with a counselor or in groups. Research indicates people feel more comfortable with this interactive computer approach. The user works with a data base which contains approximately 1,700 "screens" or pages of information, segmented into four main subject areas: financial affairs, health and lifestyle, living and occupation, and legal affairs and records.

Using FRED, the user can create a retirement program that is uniquely and entirely his or her own, and is completely confidential. Each employee receives a Planner Portfolio to record information. Two personalized disks ensure privacy and a permanent record.

The system can be customized for client employers to reflect benefits packages. It is priced on a subscription basis, with annual updates and enhancements, training for trainers, periodic newsletters and hotline assistance.

Produced by: Employee Benefit Systems, Inc.; Dr. Timothy Prynne; P.O. Box 11485; Columbia, SC 29211.

Survivors' Registry

A PC program which enables a potential retiree to build a personalized retirement plan, taking into consideration both the financial and lifestyle aspects of retirement.

This computer program stores and permits updating of personal or family assets, and permits an individual to review "what if" scenarios by varying the assumptions on income, expenses, etc.

Based upon a future retiree's projected lifestyle, the program produces income and expense projections. Comfort factor to compensate for unforeseen events and to estimate life expectancy can be selected.

The program helps a retiree build a detailed listing of assets, which can be used by the retiree's executor to close the estate. Confidentiality of data is maintained.

Survivors' Registry has the following capabilities:

1. Basic information can be maintained and easily updated regarding personal data, veteran information, burial requests and location of an individual's will.
2. Accounting, tax and estate planning information for all of an individual's assets is captured and can be modified as necessary.
3. Information on liabilities is maintained for updating. This allows

you to calculate your current net worth.

4. Income and expense by designated categories is captured to allow calculation of an individual's estimated savings for a given year. This information is then used to project the user's net worth at retirement.
5. Additionally, income and expense during retirement years is captured and retained. When this data is coupled with the parameters of: When is retirement anticipated? What is one's life expectancy? What inflation rate is anticipated? Once these factors are entered, the program then projects the net worth required to sustain the lifestyle desired in retirement.
6. The net worth projected as being required to retain the desired lifestyle in retirement is then compared to the net worth projected as being available at retirement. This provides a reasonable estimate of whether the individual can afford to retire at the time projected and in the lifestyle desired.

Alterations to reflect additional income, lifestyle variations, etc. can be projected and their effect upon the user's financial picture at retirement is calculated and displayed. The retiree then selects and saves the scenario which best reflects current planning. Additional alternatives can always be examined.

Produced by: Survivors' Registry; Chuck Tellalian; Box 265; 9582 Hamilton Ave., Huntington Beach, CA 92646.

LifeMate

LifeMate is an Information Recording and Storage System of vital family data, available for continual reference. Offered as a 3-ring notebook system or as a Hypercard version for Macintosh computers.

LifeMate can help any retiree organize data regarding business and legal affairs, health care, home, insurance, personal possessions and family matters.

We recently had the opportunity to review this system, in both the 3-ring, 96-page binder version, separated into six areas of vital data, and the Hypercard version for the Macintosh family of computers.

The latter requires Hypercard version 2.0 or higher, with 1 megabyte of RAM. The program comes on a 3.5" disc, with a complete user manual.

Either version provides a retiree with a structured way of organizing all vital data on insurance, finances, legal matters, property owned, etc. in a readily-retrievable format.

Available from LifeMate Information Storage and Retrieval System, LifeMate Systems, Inc., 1106 Willow Bottom Drive, Columbia, MD 21044.

RETIRE, RESIDE, & ETS

by Douglas Borden

RETIRE

Martlet, Inc. of Herndon, Virginia has developed a line of computer software to help those planning retirement or relocation to find a good retirement location and a good housing development in that location. The programs: RETIRE, for Locations; RESIDE, for Specific Developments, and ETS, for Military Retirees. Each is described below.

RETIRE conducts a dialog with one or two users to determine their preferences in the following areas of concern: Climate & Environment, Housing Cost, Cost of Living, Health Concerns, Senior Services, Recreation, and Nearness to Relatives & Friends.

A single user may select up to four concerns at one time. Submenus provide more detailed selections. RETIRE then evaluates the answers and provides a list of up to 30 Recommended Retirement Locations, with those most highly recommended listed first. If a printer is attached, a printout of the concerns selected and the locations recommended is provided for later study.

RETIRE is unique in that two people, such as a husband and wife, or two individuals who want to live together, may each enter one or two individual concerns and the program will reconcile the answers in listing places which might be agreeable to both persons as much as possible.

RETIRE is available as a copyrighted and copy-protected 5 1/4" or 3 1/2" disk for use on any IBM or compatible personal computer operating DOS of 2.0 or greater at $39 for a Personal Use Disk or $79 for a Multiple Users Disk. All disks are Password protected but the Multiple Use Disks will run longer before the password expires and the user will receive FREE updates for one year. For $300 a Non-copy-protected disk is available with no password protection. This may be copied for use in several offices and will not expire.

This package also includes free updates for one year and is good for users such as retirement counsellors who conduct seminars or presentations in several offices and by many people. At present, RETIRE is being updated almost monthly and the present 2.9 version is greatly improved both for speed of operation and for accuracy over earlier versions.

Since Martlet's programs are targeted for an older population, many potential users are not computer literate and do not want to try even the simplest programs themselves. For these people, Martlet has developed a Retire Personal Questionnaire, which consists of two pages of simple questions to determine the user's interest in each of the Areas of Concern mentioned above. This questionnaire is not copyrighted and it may be copied. Users fill out the form and send it to Martlet for processing. A fee of $10 is charged to individuals and $15 to couples for the processing, with each person filling out a separate questionnaire. Martlet then returns a printout of several computer runs listing recommended locations.

RETIRE was written in Turbo Pascal and when changed from Turbo 3 to Turbo 4, a greater increase in operating speed was obtained. At present RETIRE lists only about 430 locations from all over the U.S., selected from hundreds of good retirement locales. Many of these places are rural or in small towns which offer lower cost of living and housing, a more leisurely life with good recreation, and reasonable health care nearby. Some large cities and suburbs are listed and when RETIRE adds the Size of Town to its Concerns, one can select a city or a rural area.

Future versions of RETIRE will include some recommended locations in Canada since not only Canadians, but many Americans find these attractive. The data files may be expanded so that separate files will cover Eastern U.S., Central U.S., and Western U.S. Martlet learned long ago that many people do not consider the Sunbelt to be their ideal place to live, so they have included places in other parts of the country.

The RETIRE User Manual is on the disk and may be read by entering "DOC", which will display it one screen at a time. The submenus ask for specific likes and dislikes about living near Mountains, the Seashore, Lakes, Woods, Desert, etc. as well as preferences for Dry or Moist Climate, Sunbelt, Mild 4-Season Weather, or the Uniform Temperatures and Low Humidity of Southern California coast.

Housing Cost and Cost of Living present ranges and the user selects that which applies to him or her. Health Care offers choices ranging from "Complete Medical Care with Teaching Hospitals and Medical Experts" down to "Walk-In Clinics and minimal Health Care." Obviously, a person selecting a very remote area must be aware that medical services may be limited or distant.

Similarly, Senior Services vary from place to place. Some small towns which cater to retired people have excellent senior services while some large cities which have much to offer foster other concerns. Martlet does not provide any guarantee on its recommendations as the information changes constantly, and place ratings may vary over time.

Recreation is an item of great interest to many younger retirees. The listings include both Outdoor and Indoor Recreation, then each separately, and finally one which includes Entertainment and Culture.

Nearness to Friends & Relatives is important as many retirees want to live within a day's drive of their family, if not in the same town. Many people want to leave their expensive and frantic suburbs but still want to be nearby. Martlet has tried to provide places within 500 miles of the state selected and is now revising the system's logic to give more weight to certain sectors. Thus, one selecting Pennsylvania and asking to the near the Shore and within 150 miles of the mountains will get places in New Jersey and Virginia and the Carolinas as well as places in Maine.

When users find they are getting no answers at all or a very limited number, they should broaden their responses. If a person asks for a Uniform Climate (Southern California Coast) and also asks for Housing under $60,000 he won't find much, but if he asks for a Mild 4-Season Climate and Housing under $60,000 he may get places in the Ozarks or in the Appalachian Mountains, which are generally nice.

A RETIRE Demo disk is available which is similar to the regular disk except that the password expires after about 25 runs. A RETIRE promotion disk is being developed which will present a continuously-running dialog of a typical couple running the program to resolve their differences.

RESIDE

RESIDE is a new Martlet program which lists Specific Retirement Developments in particular locations. This is not on the market yet but a RESIDE Demo disk is available on request which shows how the program operates. Fictitious names are used which in the real program are replaced by all the retirement developments we have listed in that area. If a person has used RETIRE and has decided on a few locations to look at, he or she can turn to RESIDE and find out what places are listed there. Information on these places is provided by sponsors of the developments, therefore Martlet does not guarantee the accuracy of the information although in the future checks will be made to verify accuracy.

In RESIDE, places are listed by Categories: Non-Profit Places (such as Church-Related homes and some Life-Care or Continuing-Care Communities), and For-Profit Places such as Retirement Villages, Golf-Country Club Complexes, Luxury Retirement Condos or Hotels, etc. An indication of the size and nature of the development (High-rise, Patio Homes, Individual Homes, Apartments, etc.) and the cost is given. For some, there is an "entrance fee", for some there is outright purchase and for many, there is a monthly fee. All vary in the amount of investment required and the amount that may be recovered if one leaves.

RETIRE has been marketed through direct mail sales following ads or press releases in local or national papers or magazines. RESIDE will be principally marketed by use of telecomputing networks including Compuserv and Source.

ETS

ETS, (END TERM OF SERVICE) is another Martlet retirement program designed for military retirees. These constitute two different groups, those completing 20–30 years of active duty, most of whom are in their 40s or 50s, and who need good jobs, good school, inexpensive housing, but who still want to live near a military base where they can enjoy commissary, exchange, medical and recreational services. The second group are retiring Reservists and Guardsmen who have completed at least 20 years of satisfactory reserve time and are retiring at age 60. Many of these people have civilian or civil service pensions and their needs are like the regular civilian retirees except that they also want to be near a military base.

Available from Martlet Inc., P.O. Box 37, Herndon, VA 22070.

BOOKS FOR RETIREMENT PLANNERS

Executive Retirement Management: A Manager's Guide to the Planning and Implementation of a Successful Retirement

by Jack J. Leedy, M.D. and James Wynbrandt
reviewed by Marion E. Haynes

Executive Retirement Management is divided into 6 parts which include 14 chapters and 2 appendixes. The parts are:

   I. Executive Retirement: The Career Connection
  II. The Corporeal Corporation: Foundation for a Successful Retirement
 III. The Retirement Transition
 IV. Managing Your Health
  V. Early Retirement
 VI. After Retirement

According to the authors, *Executive Retirement Management* offers a complete, step-by-step guide to transition from the workplace to retirement, focusing on the emotional aspects of retirement and the rewards to be had by applying years of management experience to the retirement process. This book does not dwell on financial issues and Social Security benefits. Instead, it helps readers examine themselves, their needs and goals in retirement, and the multitude of options in second careers and retirement pursuits that await them.

The authors represent an interesting alliance of talent. Dr. Leedy is a psychiatrist while Mr. Wynbrandt is a journalist. As a result, the book is well written and deals with issues not found in the typical book on retirement. For example, there is an excellent discussion of the stages of retirement transition—Realization, Acceptance, Disengagement and Separation—and the negative emotions of retirement—fear, anger, rejection and grief.

I read the book twice, two months apart, in order to check out my first reaction. The second reading confirmed the first: Chapters 2 through 7 should either be left out or substantially reworked. These chapters deal with management personalities, management skills and organizing one's retirement along the lines of eight different corporate models. The material is not well integrated and much of the nitty-gritty "how-to" dealt with in other chapters is missing.

On the other hand, the material in Chapter 1 and Chapters 8 through 14 flows very nicely and addresses, on a practical level, the basic issues one faces as retirement approaches. For example, Chapters 8 and 9 in Part III take the 4 stages of transition from Chapter 1 and present very practical, helpful suggestions on how to handle the transition to retirement at both office and home. It includes such advice as how to write one's retirement announcement, the retirement celebration, cleaning out the office and handling the last day in the office.

Part IV, Managing your Health, is very good. It looks at three basic issues—attitude, fitness and nutrition. It does a good job of encouraging a healthful life style.

Part V looks at early retirement from both a voluntary and involuntary perspective. In today's environment, with average retirement age running from 58 to 62, depending upon the company, early retirement is a very real issue. Chapters 13 and 14 do a good job of identifying the issues one needs to take into account.

Both appendixes are quite valuable. The first critiques retirement planning programs and recommends an outline for a worthwhile program. Everyone either presenting or contemplating a retirement planning program could benefit from this information. The second appendix is a glossary of terms germane to retirement benefit plans. It is of tremendous help in understanding the jargon of benefits analysts.

Overall, I recommend *Executive Retirement Management*. The valuable information in Chapters 1 and 8 through 14 outweigh the distraction of Chapters 1 through 7. The exercises which accompany the text make the book valuable for self-study as well as group discussion. Additionally, everyone responsible for retirement counseling will better understand the feelings of their clients after reading this book.

Available from Facts on File Publications, New York and Oxford, 266 pages, hardcover, $24.95.

From Here to Retirement: Planning Now for the Rest of Your Life

by Paul Fremont Brown
reviewed by L. Malcolm Rodman

Paul Brown, a member of ISRP's Northern California Chapter, is a retired professional engineer who has followed several occupations in retirement, including that of writer, financial consultant and conductor of pre-retirement seminars.

He has used all of his "second careers" in writing this breezy, readable overview of what pre-retirement planning means to the average mature adult.

His approach is that of a retiree, who sincerely wants others to learn from his mistakes, and ultimate successes in retirement. As such, this book is useful as a workbook for pre-retirement seminars, or as a general introduction to the field.

Following an overview chapter, the book devotes about 40 pages to a broad outline of financial planning, pensions, Social Security and other money matters. With these essentials out of the way, Paul Brown writes movingly about the transition trauma, loss of identity and psychological problems occasioned by retirement.

Most retirement advice, he notes, is dispensed by individuals who have not yet retired, and cannot know how acute these adjustments might be. Drawing upon his own experience, plus those cited in brief, anonymous case histories, he explores the steps needed to create new attitudes and survive the trauma of transition.

Writing about his own retirement: "Yesterday, I wielded power and basked in the recognition that went with my position as Manager of Quality Assurance. Now it was as though I didn't exist. The things that once identified me to other people as Manager of Quality Assurance were suddenly gone—my office, my identification badge, my secretary. I didn't belong to the club anymore. I had been disconnected, drummed out of the service with only a farewell party . . . It was as if I had lost my validity as a person."

The author contends that inadequate attention is paid in pre-retirement planning programs to overcome this identity crisis and to plan for the rest of one's life.

The book offers several formulae and checklists for considering career and leisure options. Its concluding chapters cover health and wellness, leisure choices, and strategies for keeping a marriage alive and vibrant during retirement years. It ends with notes and a 3-page bibliography.

From Here to Retirement makes a contribution because the author, as a retiree, is so convincing in portraying the agonies of retiring, then offering hope that they can be overcome with proper advance preparation.

Available from Word Books, Waco, TX, 1988, 228 pages, softcover.

The Fifteen Factors of Retirement Success

by Richard Johnson, Ph.D. and Warren Jensen, D.Min.
reviewed by John Migliaccio

Richard Johnson and Warren Jensen, co-directors of the Center for Retirement Success in Des Moines, Iowa, are to be congratulated not only for producing this essential book for every ISRP member's library, but providing a valid, practical tool for use by both pre-retirees and professionals in the field as well.

The book, and accompanying Retirement Success Profile assessment instrument, are the culmination of over eight years of serious research, validation and refinement. Both are pioneering efforts on informing us about the complex nature of retirement and providing the next (usually neglected) step of making it a reality in black and white.

Each of the fifteen major chapters is formatted in the same way: A brief definition of the factor with a plain language discussion of what it is and what it means; how the factor relates to retirement; a personal assessment about expectations and personal behaviors regarding the factor; strategies and recommendations for change, if needed; and a listing of suggested resources for exploring the specific factor further. Mini case studies, examples, and anecdotes are interspersed throughout each chapter. While not all are effective, and some tend to oversimplify, they make the book's concepts very assessable for the lay reader.

There are two key aspects to Johnson's work which make the book and profile particularly useful. One is clearly identifying and explaining the factors shown to be instrumental to a successful retirement, derived empirically from extensive research and literature review on retirement.

They are: Work Disengagement; Attitude toward Retirement; Directedness (i.e., personal decision-making style); Health Perceptions; Financial Security; Life Meaning (i.e., life purpose and significance); Leisure interests; Adaptability (i.e., personal flexibility); Identification with Past Life Stages; Dependents (i.e., support needed by children, grandchildren, spouse, aging parents, etc.); Familial and Marital Issues; Perception of Age; and Replacement of Work Functions.

The second is that it explores both "expectations" (i.e., attitudes and perceptions) of the factor and "present behavior."

This crucial distinction between attitude and behavior is generally neglected in most research on retirement, yet psychologists have long recognized that both are intertwined in making effective life choices.

The authors' strong clinical counseling and experience as practitioners is evident throughout the book. Both have been active in corporate and group preretirement preparation programs, as well as individual counseling for many years, and their supportive approach in personal retirement decision-making provides a good model for anyone involved in the planning process.

The availability of the Retirement Success Profile assessment makes the concepts and examples in the book itself concrete for the individual.

The instrument contains 120 questions measuring both the expectations and behavior on each of the fifteen factors. Each pre-retiree gets an individual, computer-scored, profile comparing his or her attitudes and behavior on each factor, a personal 20-page report explaining the scores, and a comparison to others who have taken the RSP, thereby providing important "normative" data to the preretiree, and hopefully the beginning of a normative database on retirement for future analysis. Differing forms are available for married workers, single workers and non-employed spouses.

The fact that the RSP has demonstrated at least acceptable levels of validity and reliability when examined from a technical standpoint should be very reassuring to the retirement planner and the pre-retiree alike.

Since it's the only instrument specifically oriented to retirement planning which has undergone at least minimal technical measurement scrutiny, it serves as a worthwhile professional tool for corporate retirement planning programs and the individual planning professional. The RSP continues to undergo further analysis and validation, so future versions will provide an even stronger basis for its use in conjunction with retirement planning.

Available from Kendall/Hunt Pub. Co., Dubuque, IA, 1989, softcover, 205 pages, $12.50.

From Work to Retirement

by Marion E. Haynes
reviewed by L. Malcolm Rodman

Mr. Haynes is president of the International Society of Retirement Planning. He retired from the Shell Oil Company in Houston in 1991, concluding a 35-year career in human resources management. At retirement, he was the Manager of Pensioner Relations for the company, maintaining contact with thousands of Shell Oil retirees.

An author, consultant and lecturer, he has written six previous books on management and human resource subjects. He notes that his own experience in planning and implementing his own retirement contributed to the development of the book.

Writing from his long-time experience in working with retirees, Mr. Haynes has written a manual which concentrates on that important phase of a retiree's life: the period of making a successful transition from work to retirement. Such a transition, if handled properly, will prepare a retiree for years, even decades, of peace of mind and feelings of self-worth.

The book begins with a short overview of the realities of retirement today. Mr. Haynes writes: "Ideas about retirement are changing. It is no longer a relatively short period of time, when you can walk in the park, doze before a fire, fish or play a few rounds of golf. Today, retirement can span a third or more of your lifetime and offer unlimited opportunities for fulfillment."

He notes that the work ethic is ingrained in all of us. ". . . Work is an enjoyable experience for most people. It is this significance of work in your life that makes the transition to retirement so challenging."

He then describes the transition to retirement in four distinct phases which should begin long before the final day on the job. He defines each of these phases—acknowledgement, acceptance, disengagement and redefinition—and suggests how a pre-retiree should progress through them to overcome negative emotions and to prepare for a new phase of one's life.

He discusses the negative emotions associated with retirement, which must be overcome lest they lead to depression and nonproductivity. Among these negative emotions are grief, feelings of rejection, fear, anger and guilt—not unlike the feelings of someone coming down with a fatal disease. It's no wonder that psychologists classify retirement as one of the most traumatic experiences an individual can experience in a lifetime.

The book is useful as a workbook on career transition since it contains worksheets, do-it-yourself questionnaires, checklists, exercises and assessment sheets designed to walk an individual through the transition process.

The bulk of the book is devoted to a detailed examination of the choices an individual has in planning an active retirement.

These options begin with income producing activities, including full or part-time careers, consulting or owning a small business.

The choices described then progress through other activities, including volunteer service, leisure activities, hobbies, educational activities and athletics.

Each chapter briefly outlines a possible activity or course of action and lists the names and addresses of agencies where the reader can obtain additional information.

For example, the section on volunteer service directs the reader to coordinating agencies such as the National Volunteer Center and ACTION, and to specialized agencies such as the Family Friends Project of the National Council on Aging, Court Appointed Special Advocates, AARP's Legal Counsel for the Elderly, the Peace Corps and the Service Corps of Retired Executives (SCORE).

The concluding chapters contain many of the assessment tools one would encounter if they consulted a career counselor, such as a skills inventory, a risk taking quiz and a family relationship assessment form.

It concludes with the format for writing one's own retirement plan, with goals in six major areas, action steps to be taken to reach the goal, and target dates. The stated intent is to help pre-retirees answer this crucial question: "What do you want to do with your retirement?"

The book will be useful as a supplemental tool for financial planners, since it concentrates on the important non-financial aspects of a transition to retirement. Thus, it will supplement a financial planner's counsel on investments, budgeting, taxes and the like.

This volume is an important addition to every retirement planner's library. More importantly, it is a valuable tool for informing and counseling individuals preparing for retirement.

Available from Crisp Publications, Inc., Menlo Park, CA, 1993, 242 pages, softcover, $12.95.

The Best of Times

by Anita Smith
reviewed by Marion E. Haynes

I challenge you to read this book without a lump in your throat or tear in your eye. Ms. Smith successfully captures and conveys the emotions of the ten people she profiles. From their experiences, she illustrates her premise that the senior years can be the best of times.

The Best of Times is written in two parts—Book I and Book II. Book I profiles the experiences of ten people ranging in age from 68 to 84. Book II presents the insights of nine experts on aging. Chapters in Book II are "Planning for Your Retirement", "Getting Involved" and "Taking a Positive View of Your Senior Years". Let's look at these two parts more closely.

The ten individuals profiled in Book I are actively involved with life. A few have faced severe adversity, such as ill health or the loss of a spouse, but they all have found a niche where they experience fulfillment. Each one's niche is highly personal. It ranges from volunteer service to travel, playing golf and education. Here are three examples.

Ida Moffett at age 84 is enjoying a second career as Chief of Nursing Emeritus at the Ida V. Moffett School of Nursing at Stamford University. She retired from her first career at age 68 to spend time with her husband of 40 years. They enjoyed three years together until his death of a heart attack. Five years later, at age 73, Mrs. Moffett returned to full-time employment. Mrs. Moffett summarizes her experience. "I still miss Howard. I always will. Although I made some progress in dealing with my grief after Howard's death, it was having the opportunity to go back to work that really gave me a full life again. People have to find their own way, but I think it's important to become busy, active after a loss. For me, I had to have something that I felt I was really doing for someone else."

Rudy Woods retired at age 62 from his nursing career in the burn unit of the University of Michigan Hospital. He now lives in Birmingham, having chosen to return to his roots in retirement. Today, at age 69, Mr. Woods spends his time serving as a hospice volunteer, teaching others to read and reading the books he couldn't find time for while working. He says he feels good and is content with his life. He says there are four areas which can make or break a person's retirement years—health, finances, attitude toward getting older and

activities. He has paid careful attention to each of these areas in his own life.

Her name is Clifford McKissick and, at age 79, she is living her life to its fullest. However, it hasn't always been that way. Following the death of her husband ten years ago, Mrs. McKissick suffered severe depression. For 37 years, they had loved each other deeply and become very dependent upon each other. Feeling lost and alone, she didn't go anywhere, couldn't face people and thought that she too would die soon. She spent her time sitting at home, piecing quilts and thinking negative thoughts.

Finally, an assertive friend said, "I'm going to drive to your house and get you and take you to the recreation center." This was the turning point in her recovery. She says, "If people had not encouraged me, I think I likely would have gone ahead and passed on."

Today, her regular schedule is to help at the West End Nutrition Center on Mondays and Fridays, go to ElderGarden Senior Center on Wednesdays and do volunteer work at Cooper Green Hospital on Tuesdays. Thursdays are reserved for visiting sick and shut-in neighbors.

The nine experts used as a resource in Book II are all involved with older adults. From their various perspectives, they offer advice on how to prepare for your later years.

Chapter 11 is on "Planning for Your Retirement." Five keys are highlighted—health, finances, home environment, legal aspects and getting involved. An important section of this chapter deals with confronting your retirement. Here, one of Ms. Smith's experts encourages you to acknowledge the reality of retirement and prepare for the change that it will bring to your life.

Chapter 12, "Getting Involved", is the theme chapter of the book. All of the cases profiled and all of the expert advice points to the importance of being involved in something of interest to you as the key to a long, fulfilling life. This chapter identifies a variety of ways to get involved and points to specific agencies and organizations which can help. The ways to get involved summarize the experiences of the individuals profiled in Book I.

Chapter 13 encourages you to take a positive view of your senior years. Following a review of longevity data, ways for older people to contribute are reviewed. The chapter includes advice on acknowledging the emotional needs of older adults and suggests three ways to approach the senior years—reaching in, reaching out and reaching up.

It closes with the observation that if you have adequate financial resources and are in relatively good health, what you can accomplish today is limited only by your imagination.

For 20 years, Ms. Smith has reported on health news for *The Birmingham News*. Her background is evident in her writing style.

On the one hand, she captures the human side of the people she writes about.

On the other hand, there is a lot of information reported without drawing strong, organized conclusions from the information. The result is a book that I classify as more inspirational than educational.

I recommend the book. You will be touched by the people you meet and you will learn from the experts. I suggest you read the second part Book II, first. Then, read the individual stories reported in Book I.

Available from The Best of Times, Inc., Birmingham, AL, 1989, 362 pages, hardcover, $19.95.

A Field Guide to Retirement

by Alice and Fred Lee
reviewed by Marion E. Haynes

Alice and Fred Lee worked seven years researching and writing their *Field Guide to Retirement*. The result is a catalogue of options for a successful retirement.

The central theme of the book is to describe in detail 14 lifestyle opportunities for retirees. These are:

1. Staying Put in the Community
2. Wintering in the Sun Belt
3. Hitting the Road in a Recreation Vehicle
4. Retirement Area Living
5. Resort/Vacation Community
6. Large Retirement Village/City
7. Total Planned Community
8. Small Retirement Community
9. Pau Hana in Hawaii
10. Foreign Retirement
11. Special Interests
12. Retirement Residence
13. Retirement Complex with Available Health Care
14. Continuing Care/Life Care Community

As I read the book, I began to think of these options as settings or environments in which to pursue retirement interests rather than lifestyles. Because, within each setting, retirees can pursue different lifestyles. However, the Lees make a very important point. That is, you must choose a setting that is compatible with your interests in order to have a successful, fulfilling retirement. Don't get caught in the trap of moving without carefully considering what you will do at your new location to be happily involved with living.

The Lees have structured their book to help the reader choose a retirement lifestyle. The first three chapters raise questions and offer ideas on what is necessary for a successful retirement. Included in Chapter 3 is a list of 75 activities to help you generate ideas of what to pursue in your retirement. The book closes with questionnaires to guide you in identifying a lifestyle preference and developing a plan to achieve it.

The book is packed with specific information and recommendations. Take the special interest option as an example. This chapter presents collegiate, religious, and retired military facilities in detail, as well as comments on fraternal organizations and nudist retirement communities. Nine college or university affiliated retirement centers are reviewed, along with three religious affiliated and five facilities for retired military or their widows. In most cases, actual costs are reported along with a description of the facilities and privileges offered to their residents. Each of the other lifestyle options is examined in similar detail. And, the appendix contains approximately 300 addresses of places to write for information.

A Field Guide to Retirement is a valuable resource book. It is the first book to examine different options available to retirees by looking at the places they may choose to live. The Lees have visited hundreds of retirement communities, villages and facilities. Their insights as well as those of the people they talked with highlight the pros and cons of each choice.

I highly recommend *A Field Guide to Retirement* as a resource for those involved in retirement planning as well as a handbook for those nearing retirement.

Available from Doubleday, New York, 1991, 317 pages, softcover, $12.95.

Retirement Careers: Combining the Best of Work & Leisure

by DeLoss L. Marsh
reviewed by Marion E. Haynes

DeLoss Marsh is dedicated to helping the retired person identify, select, and find a compatible retirement career by examining options, opportunities, and defining those situations unique to each retiree. Whether your career in retirement is an extension of your life's work, a way to supplement income, a manifestation of a long time hobby or interest, or a totally new experience, this book can help you choose from the options available to you.

Much has been written to guide the retiree toward a financially secure retirement. Yet, financial security is not enough. One needs the stimulus of a meaningful existence to be a whole person. You need to satisfy your psychological needs, those needs that drive us all toward our own level of self-worth and well being. That's what this book is about.

Retirement Careers is an excellent starting place to begin looking at the options open to you in retirement. It will broaden your perspective and direct you to other information. It has an extensive bibliography and resource list.

Available from Williamson Publishing, Charlotte, VT, 1991, 191 pages, softcover, $10.95.

Achievers Never Quit

by Robert O. Redd
reviewed by Marion E. Haynes

According to Mr. Redd, "Achievers can't quit. They thrive on attaining new goals: building a book case or building a business; restoring an antique car or teaching adults to read." Not everyone is an achiever. But, for those who are, this book offers some very worthwhile guidance in planning later-years' activities.

Achievers Never Quit is divided into 12 chapters and a conclusion. In the first five chapters, Mr. Redd makes a case for taking control and mapping your own strategy. These chapters take little time as they contain a total of only 22 pages. Chapter 6 asks the question, "What do you really want to do?" The following chapters consider the options of conducting a job search, establishing a consulting practice, establishing a business, getting involved in education as either student or teacher, and mixing volunteer

activities and leisure. The final chapter looks at goals, action plans and timetables.

Mr. Redd provides specific help in implementing each of the options presented. For example, a resume outline and samples are included in Chapter 7 and financial forms are included in Chapter 9. Check lists and questionnaires supplement the text throughout. Specific experiences of nine individuals are included as examples of how real people have confronted real life experiences and come out winners.

In the book's conclusion, Mr. Redd observes a common thread running through the lives of the achievers he interviewed. These people are driven by a desire to enrich the lives of others. This desire gives them an unlimited source of energy, enthusiasm and self esteem. This is an interesting observation. Mr. Redd starts from the premise that certain people "thrive on attaining new goals" and must build opportunity for satisfying this need into their retirement activities. However, in conclusion, it was not the attainment of new goals but the desire to enrich the lives of others that provided the motivation for these activities. I found this troublesome, although most readers probably will not notice it.

This book is well worth its modest $4.95 price tag. While it is a bit superficial and lacks academic rigor, it has a valuable message and some very worthwhile information. I recommend it to all who are wrestling with the question of what to do with the rest of their life.

Available from Thornapple Publishing Co., Ada, MI, 1989, 133 pages, softcover, $4.95.

How to Care for Your Parents: A Handbook for Adult Children

by Nora Jean Levin
reviewed by Marion E. Haynes

Ms. Levin writes from personal experience. The result is a very practical, well organized, concise handbook for those facing the need to help their aging parents. Three major tasks are identified and dealt with: planning for legal and financial incapacities; managing income and expenses; and arranging long term care.

How to Care for Your Parents assumes you're stepping in for the first time. To guide you through the process, the book is divided into two major parts. Part I, Getting Organized, takes you through the eight steps involved in creating a personal profile, the seven steps involved in creating a financial profile and the four steps involved in plugging into community networks. Part II, Making Decisions, leads you through health insurance, long term care, in-home safety and care and housing options. These two major parts are supplemented by an introduction and a final chapter for the care giver on balancing needs of parents, immediate family, self and employment.

Ms. Levin has packed a lot of valuable information into a small package. Her writing style is clear and direct.

She takes you methodically through 28 steps in caring for your parents. Along the way, worksheet formats are provided for organizing important data. Also, the book provides names, addresses and phone numbers of sources of additional information as well as references to relevant supplemental reading material.

In the author's words, "This handbook is designed to help you to avoid the fear and stress in caring for your parents, and to save you some time and money while doing so." If you do all the things described in the book, you will be successful in achieving that objective. At $4.95, it is a real bargain.

Available from Storm King Press, Washington, DC, 1987, 103 pages, softcover, $4.95.

The Family CAREbook

edited by Dennis E. Kenny and Elizabeth N. Oettinger
reviewed by Marion E. Haynes

The editors of *The Family CAREbook* have assembled an impressive list of 15 contributors, all of whom are experienced in their area of contribution. This results in practical advice on 28 topics affecting the elderly.

The book is sub-titled "Understanding the Needs of Older Parents and How to Help." This underscores the direction it takes as it addresses each issue. Practical steps are suggested to identify options and select a course to follow. While the focus is on one's parents, the book is also beneficial to anyone involved in providing care to the elderly. Almost everyone reading the book will find something of personal value.

The 28 issues are divided into six major categories: Threshold, Household, Health, Legal, Financial, and End of Life issues. In addition, a section on Resources, a Glossary, and forms and checklists are included.

The first section on **Threshold Issues** encourages the reader to get involved with aging parents in the planning of medical, legal and household issues. In these discussions, the parents' autonomy must be respected and decision making must be

shared. The section also includes an overview of community services for case management, nutrition, transportation, legal, home care, respite, reassurance and support groups. The section concludes with discussions on working with large agencies, getting parents to accept help and providing support and care from long distance.

The **Household Issues** section presents information on various housing options and includes several checklists for deciding which is best. There is a detailed discussion on how to make any housing choice safe for elderly occupants. Also included is a comprehensive discussion of sharing one's home with an elderly parent. The final item in this section is on improving driving skills and when one should no longer drive.

Personally, I found the section on **Health Issues** to be most comprehensive. It begins with a discussion on staying healthy, which appropriately includes exercise, diet, sleep, maintaining activities and attitude. It goes on to discuss common ailments of the elderly, home health care, medications and how to select a care facility. The discussion of common ailments is particularly helpful, with its specific suggestions of ways to deal with each disorder.

The **Legal Issues** section has information on how to select and work with a lawyer including how to access legal services on a limited budget. The core of the section is an excellent discussion on estate planning and guardianship. The concluding discussion deals with consumer fraud and how to not become a victim of illegal or unethical practices. Following the information contained in this section could save you more than the cost of the book.

The **Financial Issues** section contains information on financial planning and management, Medicare, Medicaid and private insurance. As with other sections, it is very detailed.

The **End-of-Life Issues** deals with things that often are left unsaid. For example, there are discussions on how to talk about death, concerns of the dying and handling your own grief. Also included are discussions on hospice care, working with a funeral home, planning the service and whom to notify.

The section on **Resources** is printed as a pamphlet and contains addresses and phone numbers for 33 agencies or organizations. It also includes an extensive list of recommended additional reading. This pamphlet can be ordered separately at a cost of $5.95 and is available in four different editions—National, Washington State, Tri-cities Washington, and Sno-King Washington. The **Forms and Family Notes** section is also printed as a pamphlet and is available separately for $5.95.

I do not have the privilege of sharing the editors' vision for their book. Therefore, I cannot say whether or not it is fulfilling their vision.

I believe the three-ring binder, loose leaf format drives the price up unnecessarily. If a conventional soft cover format were used, the price would be reduced, resulting in broader market appeal. However, this does not detract from the fact that it contains excellent material and is well organized.

I have not seen a better reference for anyone working with the elderly.

Available from CAREsource Program Development, Seattle, WA, 1989, 342 pages, looseleaf, $34.95.

The Unfinished Business of Living

by Elwood N. Chapman
reviewed by Marion E. Haynes

Elwood Chapman, author of *Comfort Zones,* has turned out another winner. In *The Unfinished Business of Living* he has brought together a handy guide for those caring for aging parents. It is intended to be read by both the care giver and care receiver to stimulate discussion and facilitate action.

The book professes a sound philosophy. Namely, open communication with the aging parent as active participant in decisions.

The foundation of this philosophy is the family meeting where aging parent, children and grandchildren discuss matters needing attention and then decisions being carried out by those most able to do so. This includes consideration of financial means, proximity, and physical and mental ability. All participants gain through this approach.

Covering a wide range of material, Chapman describes the considerations, plans, processes, legal and social implications and other supportive steps that need to be taken to help an aging parent achieve fulfillment. He writes:

"No one completely finishes the business of living. But the amount of attention invested in loving, forgiving, bequeathing and clarifying, makes all the difference in the quality of life an older person and his or her family experience."

The book is divided into fourteen chapters. It begins with a look at the changing family and presents the case for making the care of an aging parent a family affair. Chapters are included in the emotional aspects of financial decision making etc. as well as respecting the care recipient's resistance.

A review of the legal instruments of transfer will prove very helpful to those who are not well acquainted with these matters. The chapter on community support is well worth the price of the book. The names of organizations with addresses and phone numbers will be very helpful for one just getting started in seeking help.

The chapter on care options will stimulate the reader's thinking as it guides one toward the best choice for a particular situation. Included in this chapter are tips on choosing a health care facility and an evaluation guide to help focus attention on relevant considerations and rate the facilities being considered. The chapter ends with a list of tips on visiting a loved one in a care facility.

Chapters 13 and 14 address the finishing of business most often neglected or put off. Chapter 13 discusses the practical side while chapter 14 deals with the emotional side. Examples of items discussed are: taking a "dream" trip, writing one's memoirs, renewing contacts with friends, completing the family tree, writing a letter of instructions, granting a power of attorney, putting relationships in order, and sharing feelings with loved ones.

An important feature of *The Unfinished Business of Living* is the wide array of forms, checklists, exercising and case studies presented in each chapter.

Some examples, in addition to those already mentioned, are a Family Leadership Exercise, a Communication Enhancement Exercise, a checklist on Protecting Yourself Against Stress, a Home Care Assistance Exercise, a Resistance Exercise, a Preconsultation Form to be completed before meeting with an attorney to prepare a will, plus many others.

Each chapter ends with a couple of case studies to focus discussion on the subject of the chapter. The author gives recommended responses to the cases in the appendix. Also, in the appendix, one will find a Funeral Arrangement Guide. Form letters are included which may be copied and adapted to advise the Social Security Administration and insurance companies among others of the death of a loved one. *The Unfinished Business of Living* will make a significant contribution. In addition to a personal guide and reference, it will help surface important matters for discussion when shared with aging parents. Finally, it will serve as an excellent resource and discussion guide for group study by those faced with providing care for aging parents.

Available from Crisp Publications, Inc., Menlo Park, CA, 1988, 256 pages, softcover, $10.95.

The Price Waterhouse Retirement Planning Advisor

reviewed by Marion E. Haynes

This book is packed with practical, straight-forward information to help you plan the financial dimension of your retirement. The physiological and psychological dimensions of retirement are only briefly mentioned. This is not a criticism, but rather an acknowledgment. After all, one expects Price Waterhouse to focus on financial matters.

The basic model around which the book is built is rational. You begin with a current budget and then adjust it to come up with a post retirement spending plan. This defines your income needs in retirement. Appendix I is a worksheet for developing your spending plan.

With a spending plan, the next step is to determine the investable resources needed to fund your retirement. Appendix II presents a worksheet for this purpose. Working through it, you will see the extent to which your present resources will meet your future needs. It also helps you determine how much you need to save each year to meet your retirement goal if there is a shortfall.

To help you estimate the contribution Social Security will make toward your retirement, Appendix III provides figures for both regular benefits (age 65) and early benefits (age 62).

I found the factors in the appendices to be most helpful when calculating the future value of resources, the effects of inflation and savings rates. Factor 1 is a multiplier to adjust your spending plan for 4% inflation.

You can quickly determine that in 20 years it will take $87,600 to maintain a current $40,000 spending plan. Multipliers are provided for 1 to 40 years.

Factor 2 is a multiplier to determine your capital needs at retirement. Individual multipliers are provided for estimated retirements of 20 to 40 years and at rates of return from 6% to 12%. A 4% rate of inflation is built in. With this factor you can determine that you will need $732,000 to provide $40,000 annually, in today's dollars, for 30 years, if you invest the funds at 8%.

Factor 3 shows you the capital you need to invest in order to maintain the purchasing power of your company provided pension, assuming it is not adjusted for inflation. The multipliers provided are for the same periods and rates of return as for Factor 2. For example, to maintain the spending power of a $40,000 pension with 4% inflation over 30 years would take $245,600 invested at 8%.

Factor 4 shows the rate at which your retirement nest egg will grow, tax deferred, with annual compound interest and no further capital contribution. Multipliers are provided for 1 to 40 years and at 6% to 12% annual return. With this factor, you readily see that $50,000 put away at 8% for 30 years will grow to $503,000.

Finally, Factor 5 lets you quickly determine your annual savings rate required to accumulate funds to retirement. For example, if you need to save $850,000 and have 30 years until retirement, you will have to save $7,650 annually if you invest the funds at 8%. Multipliers are given for 1 to 40 years and at 6% to 12% annual return.

From this point, the book moves to a discussion of the sources of funding for your retirement. Three are considered: Social Security, company sponsored retirement plans and personal savings. Three additional, often overlooked sources are also mentioned—tapping the equity in your home, tapping the cash in your life insurance policies and working after retirement. The next nine chapters look at investing. This part of the book is elementary. But, that is where most people need to begin. For example, stocks, bonds and mutual funds are described as well as the various stock exchanges. I found the explanations of these investment alternatives both clear and concise.

Chapter 11 examines some fundamental truths about investing. It encourages a long term strategy, diversity of investments and analysis. Real rate of return is explained as the gross rate of return less taxes and inflation.

Chapters 12 and 13 deal with risk. Chapter 12 describes six different types of risk—inflation, deflation, interest rate, market, business and illiquidity. Chapter 13 explains the relation between risk and rate of return.

It then shows how to minimize risk through asset allocation. Four asset categories are presented: cash and cash equivalents, fixed income instruments, equities and hard assets. Chapters 14 through 17 describe these categories in detail.

Chapter 18 goes into mutual funds in detail—what they are and how they work. Chapter 19 puts the asset allocation concept to use by showing how to allocate a portfolio to match your risk tolerance and income needs.

Social Security is covered in three chapters. Chapter 5 gives a good introduction to retirement and survivor benefits. An interesting point made in this chapter is how quickly you will recover all that you have paid into Social Security. For example, if you are 45 today, you will recover all the taxes you pay up to age 65 in only 5½ years after you begin drawing benefits. Chapter 20 explores when and how to apply for benefits, and Chapter 24 explains Medicare.

The book wraps up with a few miscellaneous issues like long term care insurance, paying estimated income taxes, selling your home and should you retire early. It then closes with 3 chapters on estate planning.

The Price Waterhouse Retirement Planning Advisor is an excellent investment. Its modest price makes it one of the best bargains available today. The writer has done an excellent job making a complex subject readable and understandable.

Short chapters with effective use of subheadings makes it easy to refer back to specific topics. Case studies illustrate points being made in the text.

I particularly like the way the book closes: "You and only you can make your retirement a satisfying one. Planning for your needs . . . rests solely in your hands. No company, no government, no society will do it for you."

Available from Pocket Books, a division of Simon & Schuster, Inc., New York, 1990, 374 pages, softcover; $4.95.

You Can Afford to Retire!

by William W. Parrott and John L. Parrott
reviewed by Marion E. Haynes

The authors are President and Vice President of Creative Retirement Planning, a New York financial planning and counseling service, and members of ISRP. Their stated objective in writing this book is to answer the most commonly asked questions about finances and retirement.

The book is organized into three parts. The first part addresses questions relating to income needs, taxes, inflation, retirement program options and Social Security. The second part discusses investments most commonly utilized by retirees. The authors promise a relatively new, simple and comprehensive approach to investing that will generate an average portfolio return of 9% to 11%. The third part presents four case studies.

The book begins in a logical place—a determination of retirement income needs. Two approaches are offered. One is a detailed budget method. The other is a take-home pay method. Worksheets are provided for determining post-retirement needs using either method. It is suggested that post-retirement needs should be 85% to 90% of present take-home pay. The authors then turn their attention to examining the impact of life expectancy, taxes and inflation on funding these post-retirement needs. They state that the most sensible retirement program should involve living off interest and dividends alone.

This implies that principal will be preserved and passed on to heirs. Everyone will not agree with this approach. Some people prefer to develop a program that

includes the draw down of investable resources, much like that required by IRAs.

In looking at sources of income to fund post-retirement needs, the authors discuss pensions, Social Security and financial assets. There is a comprehensive discussion of the most common options available under qualified pension plans.

This information should help the average reader make an informed decision about spousal options and lump-sum versus annuity, although the authors clearly favor a lump-sum settlement. The taxation of lump-sum distributions is well presented.

In the Social Security chapter, the authors do a good job of presenting the details of Social Security as it relates to retirement and survivors' benefits, including Medicare.

However, disability benefits are not discussed. This is unfortunate since many people retire due to disability and others who retire early qualify for disability benefits before qualifying for retirement benefits.

The chapter concludes with a look at financing nursing home care through Medicaid and long term care insurance.

The financial assets chapter provides a worksheet for preparing a personal balance sheet and income statement. As a result of this effort, the reader will have a complete inventory of assets, the income they generate, and liabilities—a good starting point for planning anyone's financial future.

Part 2, Chapters 5 through 10, explores individual investment alternatives, including the primary residence, guaranteed investments, tax-wise investments, growth investments, mutual funds and asset allocation.

After studying these chapters, the reader should have a good basic knowledge of investment alternatives and how to allocate assets among them. The strategy of asset allocation and utilizing mutual funds recommended by the authors is well accepted in the financial planning community.

They recommend Morningstar evaluations as the basis for selecting high quality mutual funds. Their counsel to look at net return rather than ignore load funds altogether makes sense. For example, Fidelity's Magellan Fund has been the top performing fund for several years and it has a 2% front end load.

The four cases in Part 3 look at couples with annual budgets of $40,000 and $70,000 and singles with annual budgets of $30,000 and $50,000. Studying these cases, in particular the one most closely approximating the reader's financial situation, will give insight into the authors' financial counseling. Specific recommendations are given to each client on repositioning investments to meet income needs.

An appendix reproduces the Value Line reports for all of the stocks mentioned in the cases. Another appendix reproduces the Morningstar reports on recommended mutual funds.

I personally don't believe it is appropriate to devote over 100 pages to this material. The examples of each contained in earlier chapters with instructions to the reader on how to obtain current reports should be sufficient. Both are available by subscription and at public libraries, banks, brokers' and financial planners' offices.

I found the book easy to read and understand. I particularly like the "Helpful Hints" scattered throughout. For example, if you earn less than the Social Security earnings limit, you should start drawing benefits at age 62.

I believe the authors met their stated objective quite well. I'm adding the book to my list of recommended reading.

Available from New York Institute of Finance, New York, 1992, 375 pages, softcover, $14.95.

Spend Your Way to Wealth

by Kathleen L. Cotton
reviewed by Marion E. Haynes

Ms. Cotton is a Certified Financial Planner, registered investment advisor and a partner in a Seattle financial planning firm. She is also an adjunct faculty member at City University and a member of ISRP. This is her third book in the financial planning field.

Planning is an essential element in many of life's endeavors. Without plans, successful results cannot be assured. Financial success is no exception. Whether your goal is retirement or financial independence, the process begins with clarifying your goals and value system.

According to the author, the book was developed as a practical and informative tool to aid readers in gaining control over their finances. She certainly hit her target. This book is practical and the most informative I've had the pleasure to review.

While the idea of spending your way to wealth is novel, it emphasizes the need to systematically spend a portion of your income on the future (commonly known as saving). Also, it causes the reader to carefully consider spending on current consumption and what part of that is discretionary spending.

Chapters 1 through 4 build a foundation of information. Chapter 5 provides a framework for clarifying goals and evaluating one's ability to achieve them based on a priority system.

Chapter 6 discusses the elements of net worth and the importance of periodically updating a net worth statement. Chapter 7 teaches the reader how to create spending solutions to common money management problems.

It's been estimated that two thirds of the population lives paycheck to paycheck. You will never be able to get ahead unless you can change this spending pattern. This chapter looks at cash flow, credit card use and debt management. Chapter 8 discusses cost-effective protection through the use of appropriate insurance.

In Chapter 9, the economics of home ownership are presented, including both primary residence and rental property. Eight reasons for home ownership are outlined, as well as how to evaluate mortgage qualifications and loan amortizations.

Chapter 10 takes the reader from categorizing assets through quantifying a portfolio

for optimum risk and return. Chapters 11, 12 and 13 describe practical investment choices in detail. After reading these chapters, the reader should understand common investment instruments, mutual funds and tax-deferred investing.

Chapters 14 and 15 focus on reducing taxes. This includes consideration of both federal income tax and federal estate tax. Tax shelters, tax shifts, tax tricks and tax traps are fully explained.

The next four chapters address the two most common financial concerns of Americans— education and retirement funding. Chapter 16 enumerates college funding strategies while Chapters 17, 18 and 19 are devoted to preretirement or "financial independence" planning.

Chapter 20 looks at five stages of adulthood defined by age and family structure. Actions and recommendations are presented for each of the stages.

The concluding Chapter 21 takes the reader through a process for choosing a financial planner. A list of 20 questions to ask a potential advisor is included. The Resource Directory in the Appendix is a valuable guide for further study.

The book is loaded with illustrations, exhibits, examples, self-evaluation questionnaires and worksheets. They help the reader internalize the information and develop his or her own set of financial records and plans.

The book is well written, easy to understand and the most comprehensive I've see. Ms. Cotton shares information on investment evaluation and asset allocation that others writing in the field have chosen to withhold. And, she does it in a way that is easily understood. Her basic wealth building approach of asset allocation and diversification is a commonly accepted approach that seems to work.

The book is written for the younger reader, since it includes considerations of home ownership and educating children. However, I found most of the book relevant to readers nearing retirement. Material that might not appear germane at first glance may in fact have something to offer. For example, the chapter on educating children has some good ideas for helping with the education of grandchildren.

I highly recommend the book as either a self-study text or as a text and reference

manual for classroom use for adults of any age, including retirement planning.

Available from Boston Books, Spokane, WA, 1992, 277 pages, softcover, $12.95.

Warning: Dying May Be Hazardous to Your Wealth

by Adriane G. Berg
reviewed by Marion E. Haynes

Ms. Berg is an estate planner and attorney who hosts a weekly radio talk show on financial matters. She has written this book to educate its readers on the array of concepts and options involved in estate planning. It is not intended as a do-it-yourself manual. Rather it prepares you to talk intelligently with an estate attorney and customize a plan to meet your unique needs.

The author observes that senior wealth is under attack. If the nursing home doesn't get your money, the tax man will. If available estate planning and preservation tools are not utilized, as much as 55 percent of your assets will go to pay federal estate taxes, and that is before the costs of probate are deducted.

While saving on estate taxes is a valid motivation to get your house in order, just as important is to see that those you select

and designate benefit from your assets when you no longer need them. An AARP brochure puts estate planning very succinctly:

You own stuff . . . You will die . . . Someone will get your stuff. Estate planning is seeing that your stuff goes to those you choose.

The book is divided into seven parts and sixteen chapters. The appendix contains a glossary, sample forms, and worksheets.

Part one discusses the details of wills, trusts, gifts, and probate. Part two shows how estate taxes are calculated and how to use some simple techniques to save nearly $200,000 in estate taxes. Part three looks at ways to build an estate and keep it in a family for several generations.

Part four discusses the role of real estate in building wealth and how to use it to save on estate taxes. Part five explores three family crises that could impact financial well-being: divorce and remarriage, and incompetent adult child, and debt. Part six gives you information on dealing with illness, incompetency, and long-term health care. Part seven discusses what to tell your family about your estate plan.

Here are some of the estate planning strategies the book teaches:

- Dynasty planning
- Legacy planning
- Traditional estate planning
- Probate avoidance
- Tax planning for middle class couples
- Tax planning for widows and widowers
- Longevity planning
- Protection of assets from liability
- Divorce protection
- Providing for adult children who can't handle finances
- Real estate
- How to talk to your parents and children about money
- Legal forms and clauses worth understanding

Ms. Berg has successfully compiled and explained in layman's terms the concepts and strategies you need to plan your estate. But, as she aptly states in the Epilogue, "All the book learning in the world will not put money in your family's pocket. This book and any like it is no substitute for taking action."

Warning: Dying May Be Hazardous to Your Wealth has wide application in retirement planning. Financial planners, estate planners, attorneys and CPA's could provide this book to clients to enhance their understanding of estate planning concepts. This would build a solid foundation from which to develop individual estate plans.

The book could also be handed out as a resource in retirement planning programs or as a text in estate planning. Finally, it could be distributed by organizations who are concerned about their members' financial well-being.

Available from Career Press, Hawthorne, NJ, 1992, 224 pages, softcover, $14.95.

Lew Altfest Answers Almost All Your Questions About Money

by Lewis J. Altfest, Ph.D. and Karen Caplan Altfest, Ph.D.
reviewed by L. Malcolm Rodman

Lew Altfest brings impressive credentials to this basic work on financial planning. He is a Ph.D., CPA and CFP and his co-author is a Ph.D. Together, they are principals of

a financial planning firm in New York City, and coincidentally, members of ISRP.

They use a question-and-answer format and a crisp, straightforward style to carry the reader through the basics of money management. They begin with questions about managing cash flow: how much of my salary should I save? How will inflation affect my savings? What records should I keep?

These are typical of the questions posed, then answered in the book. Subsequent chapters are concerned with handling credit, the basics of investing, selecting insurance, college financing, real estate and tax planning.

This takes the reader to a series of chapters dealing with retirement-related issues, including planning for retirement, setting up an estate, relationship planning and caring for elderly parents.

The chapter on retirement planning concerns itself strictly with financial questions. Typical questions posed, then answered, are concerned with IRA and tax laws, medical outlays and nursing home costs, retirement budgeting, affording early retirement and the best age to take Social Security benefits.

The book progresses to an exploration of the need for developing a financial plan, whether the reader is capable of doing so by himself, and under what circumstances might a financial planner be helpful. In appendices, the authors provide a format for constructing a financial plan, using personal balance sheets, cash flow projections and retirement savings forecasts.

They also provide formats for calculating financial needs for retirement, life insurance, disability income and college planning. In sum, the book is a well-organized and readable overview of the financial planning needs over one's lifetime.

It may suggest to readers areas where further research is needed, beyond the overview treatment provided by this book.

Available from McGraw Hill, New York, 1992, 371 pages, hardcover, $19.95.

Retirement Income on the House: Cashing In on Your Home with a "Reverse" Mortgage

by Ken Scholen
reviewed by L. Malcolm Rodman

Should a **reverse mortgage** figure in retirement planning? What are the pros and cons of a retiree continuing to live in their present home for the rest of their life, while earning monthly income from their equity?

This is a new topic, of vital interest to every retiree. You should learn all you can about this subject in order to counsel pre-retirees.

A reverse mortgage could offer them a middle ground between selling out and downsizing homes, or staying put at the possible risk of being "house poor"—having too little retirement income despite a large equity.

The **theory of the reverse mortgage** is to permit them to generate steady retirement income from the equity locked up in their homes. Yet, despite years of talk and experimentation, this is a relatively new financial product.

Fortunately for consumers, there exists the non-profit **National Center for Home Equity Conversion.** It is dedicated to promoting their adoption by financial institutions, obtaining government insurance and educating the public.

The Center recently published a manual on reverse mortgages entitled **"Retirement Income on The House".** In non-technical language, the book walks you, step by step, through the technicalities.

It begins by describing the basic concept, by comparing and contrasting this new-type of mortgage with the traditional mortgages which millions have used to finance the purchase of their homes.

With a traditional mortgage, you begin with a small equity (your down payment) and assume as substantial debt, which is paid off by monthly payments to the lender over a prescribed number of years. This is a so-called "forward" mortgage, described as a **"falling debt, rising equity"** deal, by which a client eventually owns their home free and clear.

The reverse mortgage literally reverses the process—a **"rising debt, falling equity"** concept. That is, they start with no debt and a substantial equity in their home.

They receive **monthly advances** from the lender—income to supplement retirement pensions, Social Security, etc. Since they **make no repayments, the amount they owe goes up.**

At some future time, **the deal ends** when they sell and move from the home, after a stated number of years, or when one or both spouses die (depending upon the contract). The home is sold; the lender gets his loan back, with interest; and any remaining equity is distributed according to the terms of the contract.

There are many variations to this basic concept, such as a reverse mortgage for a fixed number of years, or for the rest of your lives. There are **government-provided mortgages** to help older homeowners repair their homes or pay property taxes. Others are offered by **private lenders,** with or without government **FHA insurance.**

In every case, the lender must calculate his risk and decide upon a monthly advance to the homeowner. Factors to be considered include the age of the homeowner, the home's value, loan costs—fees, closing costs, insurance, interest on loan balance, and an estimation of how much the property will appreciate over the term of the loan.

A borrower may be short-changed if the monthly payment calculation is either too small or too generous.

The book devotes a considerable amount of space to discussing the concept of **"total loan cost" or TLC.** This is the only way to judge the attractiveness of the deal. It's not enough to calculate the loan advances (how much you'll get each month), but what you pay in costs and what you have remaining as leftover equity at the end of the deal.

There are a number of variables which require educated guess work—**actuarial calculation,** if you want to be technical. **How long will you live?** A male who lives to be 65 can expect to live 14.2 more years; a female, 18.4 years. These are statistical averages; many individuals will exceed these spans, just as others will not.

Also, both the client and the lender must guess at **inflation** and **real estate appreciation** rates in future years.

As a reverse mortgage holder, clients have certain advantages. They keep title to their home and full control over it. The lender's only recourse for recovering his loan is the value of the residence, not any other assets the client may own.

Recognizing that a reverse option is not for everyone, the book devotes a chapter to **other housing options**, including selling and moving to a smaller home, a rental unit, a congregate living facility or retirement community, or a shared housing or group home situation.

With or without a reverse mortgage, it suggests older homeowners utilize support services to help them keep their home, such as assistance with cleaning, shopping, meal preparation, yard work and maintenance, as well as at-home health care services.

The book notes that reverse mortgages are a new financial product. Improvements and new variations keep coming out, in response to consumer demand.

1992, 340 pages, softcover, $24.95 plus $4.50 shipping. Order from the National Center for Home Equity Conversion, Suite 300, 1210 E. College Drive, Marshall, MN 56258. The author is the founder and director of the nonprofit National Center for Home Equity Conversion, and is regarded as the nation's leading authority on the subject. The following article summaries the contents of this book.

Reverse Mortgage Locator—Current listing of financial institutions offering reverse mortgages in each state, giving their name and telephone number. Available from NCHEC at address shown above. Send $1.00 and a self-addressed, stamped, business-size envelope.

Social Security: What Every Taxpayer Should Know

by A. Haeworth Robertson
reviewed by Marion E. Haynes

Mr. Robertson is President and Founder of the Retirement Policy Institute which is a research and education organization devoted to the study of national retirement policy matters. Mr. Robertson was Chief Actuary for the Social Security Administration from 1975 to 1978. For the last 15 years he has written and lectured widely, giving special emphasis to interpreting and clarifying the financial status of Social Security. His first book, *The Coming Revolution in Social Security,* was published in 1981. Today, he is considered the nation's foremost authority on the topic.

Mr. Robertson's new book is written in three parts. Part One is an introduction, Part Two is basic background information, and Part Three is a commentary on selected topics. Let's look at some of the ideas he presents in greater detail.

According to the author, many of us fall into a bad habit of referring to "government responsibility" and having the "government pay" for something. Who is this "government" we look to for help?

Bureaucrats and politicians do not have any money except that collected in taxes. When a program is set up to give someone $100 in benefits, the government must do two things: 1) find someone willing to work and earn $100; and 2) convince that person that he or she should give the $100 to the government in the form of taxes.

So, actually, when we demand a benefit from the government, we are demanding it from our friends and neighbors.

This principle must be kept in mind when considering Social Security because, contrary to the perception of many, it is not an insurance funded program. The average worker retiring at age 62 recoups his contributions in 3.28 years, while the average worker retiring at age 65 recoups his contributions in only 2.54 years.

Social Security is nothing more than a promise to a group of people that their children will be taxed for that group's benefit.

Where are things headed? Some very accurate observations can be made over the next 75 years. Total expenditures are projected to grow from about 15% of taxable payroll in 1990 to approximately 18% by the year 2000, to 32% by the year 2030, and to grow somewhat more slowly thereafter, peaking at 35% in 2060. This scenario is the Intermediate Assumption. The Pessimistic Assumption produced a 2060 tax rate of about 54% while the Optimistic Assumption is about 20%.

Where will the money come from to fund this increase in benefits? If you think the Trust Fund buildup will come to the rescue, consider the following information.

In reality, there is no trust fund. Any excess payroll taxes collected over benefits paid out plus administrative costs is loaned to the treasury to cover general expenses of the government.

When these funds are needed to cover excess costs of Social Security, they won't be there—they have already been spent. Therefore, the government will have to raise taxes through some other means to pay them back. Whether this new tax is a payroll tax, an income tax, or some other form of tax, it will be paid by those working and earning at the time it is needed.

Precedent is already being established for covering the costs from general revenue.

While 98% of the cost of Old-Age, Survivors, and Disability and Hospital Insurance programs is financed by payroll tax, this is not the case with Supplementary Medical Insurance. Here 25% is paid by premiums from participants and the remaining 75% is paid by general revenue.

It is important to realize that changing the method of financing does not change the cost of Social Security. It simply spreads the cost over different groups.

Payroll taxes apply primarily to those who will eventually benefit while general revenue taxes are paid by everyone whether they participate in Social Security or not. Today 9% of Social Security benefits are paid from general revenue.

So, what is the outlook for the future? The following eight points seem to be reasonable expectations:

- Taxpayers must become accustomed to paying higher taxes unless benefits are substantially reduced.

- It seems unlikely that the payroll tax will continue to be the source of revenue for the program that it is today.

- All state and local government employees will eventually become participants in the program.

- Beginning in about 15 to 20 years workers will begin drawing benefits at a higher age.

- Social and economic changes in the nation will result in a substantial revision in the program.

- If the nation experiences high inflation, the private sector will meet less of future retirees' income needs.

- The Medicare program as well as the nation's entire health care system will be changed dramatically during the next ten years.

- Benefits will be reduced by one means or another.

This book is a must for those in retirement planning and counseling.

It goes beyond the official assurance that the Social Security program is in sound financial shape during the foreseeable future and that there is nothing to worry about. This short term view overlooks the fact that the majority of those who will draw benefits during the next 75 years are already born and therefore can be studied with a high degree of accuracy.

The book presents an easily understood analysis of the future with suggestions on what to do to prepare for it.

While the $40.00 price may scare some people off, please note that quantity discounts quickly bring the price down: 5 to 9 copies at $30.00 each, 10 to 24 copies at $25.00 each, and 25 or more copies at $20.00 each. Shipping is paid on all pre-paid orders.

Available from Retirement Policy Institute, Washington, DC, 1992, 345 pages, hardcover, $40.00.

Social Security: The Inside Story

by Andy Landis
reviewed by Marion E. Haynes

The author, an ISRP member, worked for 12 years in a number of Social Security offices before establishing his own Seattle consulting firm, Thinking Retirement, which conducts seminars and workshops on retirement and Social Security issues.

While at SSA, he developed and appeared in the agency's own retirement videotape.

This book explains the basic rules of Social Security in nontechnical language which a typical future beneficiary will understand. Separate chapters cover eligibility and the computation of retirement benefits, benefits for family members, survivors benefits, disability benefits and Medicare.

Other sections instruct on filing claims and provide a Q and A on common questions about the program.

In a series of appendices, Mr. Landis offers a sample retirement computation, facts and figures on the program and a glossary of terms.

The book is laid out with bold section headings and concise paragraphs, making it easy to use as a reference or as a seminar workbook on Social Security.

Available from Mount Vernon Press, Bellevue, WA, 1993, 320 pages, softcover, $14.95.

Retire Right: Social Security Made Simple

by Tonya J. Nieman
reviewed by L. Malcolm Rodman

Tonya Nieman, active in ISRP's Orange County chapter, is an 11-year veteran of the Social Security Administration who now operates her own pre-retirement consulting and training firm, Sixty-Two Retirement Consulting in Costa Mesa, CA.

This publication is designed as a workbook on Social Security for reference or use in retirement planning sessions.

It begins with an explanation of Social Security tax rates and eligibility requirements. It next explains retirement benefits, including early retirement and discusses how to file a claim for benefits.

It next covers rules for family-owned and incorporated businesses, delayed retirement credits, benefits for married and divorced spouses and children's benefits.

Sections explain Medicare, the notch baby issue, cost of living increases and the claims and appeal processes.

Seminar presenters will find this a useful workbook for presenting Social Security and Medicare in a meaningful way.

Available from Sixty-Two Retirement Consulting, Costa Mesa, CA, 1992, 93 pp. soft cover workbook, $12.95.

The 50 Healthiest Places To Live and Retire in the United States

by Norman D. Ford
reviewed by L. Malcolm Rodman

Author Norman D. Ford has produced a "retirement haven" work that emphasizes wellness principles and selects localities that permit a low-stress life style, outdoor living and exercise, the availability of healthy foods, alternative religions and challenges for the mind.

Not every practitioner will accept all of the author's criteria for selecting a retirement community, but it is informative to follow his reasoning.

For example, he insists on vigorous outdoor exercise for retirees. Thus, to rate with him, a town must have a well developed system of bicycle paths. And these facilities must not be just for leisurely pedaling. He seeks 10 to 35 miles of non-stop bikeways to allow brisk pedaling of 60 to 95 rpm or more on high-performance bikes with a wide range of gears.

Likewise, he looks for the availability of year-round heated swimming pools for adult lap swimming, as well as opportunities for cross country skiing, rowing, canoeing, hiking and square dancing.

His preference for learning and intellectual challenges for retirees gives his book a decided bias in favor of college or university towns.

He looks for opportunities for all forms of prayer, meditation and spiritual belief to help minimize the effects of stress and to help the body ward off diseases. This, in turn leads him to rate a community on the availability of alternative religions and health food stores.

Additionally, he looks for communities where a significant portion of the population is supportive of an active, healthful lifestyle.

These criteria lead him mainly to small towns, away from bustling cities and suburbs, and toward towns that contain a major university or college. His top five choices: Boulder, CO, Eugene, OR, Ann Arbor, MI, Madison, WI and Chapel Hill, NC—all university towns. He does choose several large cities, including San Diego and Seattle.

He disqualifies virtually all of New England and the middle Atlantic states as being too expensive—a curious omission.

On the other hand, he does not confine himself to sunbelt towns, saying constant sunshine and warmth are no guarantee of good health. Rather, he prefers localities with a mild, four-season climate without too much snow, heat waves or other weather extremes. He also advocates "terrain therapy"—living in a area where inspiring scenery provides comfort for the soul. This may be mountains, parklands, forests, deserts or sea or lake shores.

In the initial chapters of the book, the author details his criteria, including how he has constructed a measurement of a town's stressfulness rating. In the concluding portion of the book, he devotes a section to detail the attractions of his choice of each of America's 50 most healthful cities.

A typical description will begin with the population and elevation, and the town's stress rating. The description paints a word picture of the town's location, its employment and educational opportunities, its climate and exercise options, its cultural offerings and possibilities for fellowship. It details the availability of health care, the types and costs of housing and a reference to civic amenities. He ends with the address and telephone number of the local chamber of commerce, where additional information may be obtained.

A careful reading of this book will provide pre-retirees with useful concepts about the importance of a wellness program and the need to plan for the productive use of leisure time. Also, it will suggest a number of towns worth researching and visiting before one decides upon a retirement town.

Available from Ballantine Books, New York, 1992, 256 pages, softcover, $4.99.

Arthur Frommer's New World of Travel

by Arthur Frommer
reviewed by L. Malcolm Rodman

Veteran travel guide publisher Arthur Frommer set out to write a new type of travel guide to help Americans get away from the "trivial and bland" package vacations offered by most travel agents.

In the process, he has created a valuable resource book on leisure options available to mature adults, for both individual retirees and those who counsel them.

This is an impressive compilation of novel travel ideas, including new themes of travel, new methods and sponsors, and new ways to reduce travel costs. The book is organized into concise chapters—one idea per chapter. In each, the author identifies one or more sources or agencies in bold face type, including name, mailing address, telephone number and toll-free 800 number, where available.

For anyone contemplating the challenging use of leisure time, the possibilities suggested by the book are awesome. They range from vacations at consciousness-exploring "new age" resorts, to yoga ashrams to travel seminars in third world nations.

Campus vacations, in the US and abroad, are covered, along with volunteer vacations where participants work from wilderness lands in the U.S. to collective farms in Israel or archaeological sites worldwide.

Alternative lodgings are discussed, including hostels, bed and breakfast homes and private spas. One chapter explains how to bargain for a lower rate in any type hotel.

The author next identifies bargain vacation destinations worldwide, ranging from Orlando to Malta, Nova Scotia to Wales.

A substantial portion of the book is involved with travel in the mature years. It describes the extended-stay vacations offered off-season in European resorts as great retirement vacation bargains, and identifies the agencies sponsoring such trips.

Next, the book examines the four major agencies specializing in tours for seniors. It considers the pros and cons of these organizations, and suggests their tour prices are not competitive with other firms.

The author is equally uncharitable when it comes to most hotel and airline discounts, claiming in most cases the savings is merely the 10% travel agent commissions the hotels or carriers save by having the clientele deal directly with them.

Finally, the book concludes with a number of chapters advising travelers on how to save on cruises and tours by using so-called bucket shops and specialists in "distress" bookings—unsold cruise cabins or charter flight seats, just before departure.

These chapters, which might be subtitled "what your travel agent never tells you", explains how to use ethnic travel agencies to obtain discount air tickets to Asia or South America, and how to locate travel agencies which work on a fixed fee, rebating the 10% commission to the client.

As noted, each item of advice identifies the appropriate agency by name, address and telephone number. This is reinforced with additional compilations of money-savings travel sources in the Appendix, including 24 discount travel agencies, 11 reliable "distress merchants" of travel offerings; 8 leading rebators, discounting every tour, and 21 of the nation's leading discount cruise agencies.

Incidentally, we note this comprehensive volume includes a description of ISRP member Jane Parker's Retirement Explorations, which takes pre-retirees on trips to Portugal and Costa Rica to consider off-shore retirements.

The author intends to update this compilation annually, with suggestions from readers.

For anyone interested in exploring the myriad of travel and leisure options available to mature individuals, this book is a "must".

Available from Prentice Hall Trade Division, New York, 1989, 382 pages, softcover, $14.95.

The Retirement Sourcebook: Your Complete Guide to Health, Leisure and Consumer Information

by Edward L. Palder
reviewed by L. Malcolm Rodman

This is an impressive compilation of resources and information to help retirees make knowledgeable decisions in a wide variety of subject areas. It lists more than 5,000 sources of information covering more than 200 subjects.

The work is divided into five major areas of concern to retirees: consumer information;

home and family life; travel and leisure; health; and organizations and resources.

Each section is further divided by topic. The health section, for example, has sections on specific problems and ailments, ranging from alcohol abuse, through mental health problems to vision problems.

In the consumer information section, there are suggestions on obtaining assistance and information on subjects as diverse as buying an automobile or motor home to funerals, to health quackery to pensions and living wills.

Topics covered contain introductory information, followed by listings of toll-free hotlines, where to obtain brochures or books, organizations and clearinghouses for information; and finally, catalogs and product information.

The sourcebook does not attempt to provide answers, but concentrates in descriptions and ordering data for thousands of free or low-cost brochures from authoritative sources on retirement issues.

An Appendix includes a listing of all publishers mentioned in the book, with addresses and telephone numbers. There is an index of Hotlines, covering two-thirds of a page, and a listing of organizations and clearinghouses which runs 4 pages. Finally, there is a subject index.

Available from Woodbine House, Kensington, MD, 1989, 530 pages, softcover, $14.95.

Worst Pills, Best Pills

*by Sidney M. Wolfe, M.D. and the staff
of the Public Citizens Health Research Group
reviewed by L. Malcolm Rodman*

This consumer advocacy health group, affiliated with Ralph Nader, is an outspoken opponent of many medical practices which are current in the U.S. today. It believes that many Americans, especially the elderly, are prescribed too many drugs and are not told enough about the medications they are instructed to take.

This informative book is subtitled "The older adult's guide to avoiding drug-induced death or illness" and is further sub-titled, "104 pills older adults should not use and 183 safer alternatives."

It might also be sub-titled, "What your physician has neglected to tell you about your medications." The volume was compiled by a team of medical researchers, attorneys, economists and clinical pharmacists, and lists a page and a half of physician advisors who reviewed portions of the book related to their specialties.

The opening chapter sets out the thesis that older adults are prescribed too many drugs. It notes that in 1986, older Americans filled 613 million prescriptions for drugs at retail drugstores, for an average of 15.5

prescriptions per person. Representing 16.6% of the population, they take almost 40% of all prescription drugs.

It cites "mounting evidence that many of our older citizens are getting prescription drugs which are entirely unnecessary . . . or they are getting a more dangerous drug when a much less dangerous one would work, or a lower dose of the same drug would give the same benefits with lower risks."

The balance of the volume gives chapter and verse on specific drugs, organized by treatment regimes. For example, there are sections on heart, blood pressure and blood vessel drugs. Another on mind drugs, including tranquilizers, sleeping pills, antipsychotics and antidepressants. It goes on to painkillers and arthritis drugs, gastrointestinal drugs, etc.

Each section explains general families of drugs. For example, in the section on painkillers and arthritis drugs, it explains three classes of drugs: aspirin and salicylates, narcotics, and arthritis and inflammation drugs.

It proceeds to list each drug by both generic and trade name, and in outline form advises what to do before using the drug, when to use, how to use it, what interactions might take place with other drugs, possible adverse effects and periodic tests which may be needed when taking the drug.

In some cases, a drug is identified with a black boxed "Do Not Use" warning, and the reasons are spelled out. In some cases, the warning applies specifically to older adults; in others it is a general wave-off, or it might be noted "The FDA has concluded that this drug lacks evidence of effectiveness."

In some cases, it will recommend "Limited Use."

For each section, it lists drugs considered "okay." For example, in the arthritis section, it approves of aspirin, ibuprofens and enteric-coated aspirin over more exotic and expensive drugs. And it flatly warns "do not use" for some widely prescribed ones.

This book should be especially useful for individuals who are being prescribed different drugs by different physicians. It emphasizes the dangers of drug interactions and the need to have a primary care doctor coordinate one's care and drug use.

Living with aches and pains is an unfortunate by-product of growing older. So is the taking of countless medications. *Worst Pills, Best Pills* makes an important contribution in helping older adults become more knowledgeable about the drugs they take.

Available from Public Citizens Health Research Group, Washington, D.C., 532 pages, softcover, $12.00.

10

APPENDIX

International Society for Retirement Planning

Board of Directors—1995

President
Eric J. Berry
Office of Services to the Aging
State of Michigan

Vice President
Jacquelyn Larson-Kelley
Retirement Planning and Gerontology
  Consultant

Treasurer
Steven S. Shagrin, CFP
Vice President
Smith Barney

Past President
Marion E. Haynes
Manager Pensioner Relations (Ret.)
Shell Oil Company

Directors
Victor N. Claman
President
Insights, Inc.

Jane W. Cooper
Senior Training Consultant
The Equitable

Clare B. Corbett
Retirement Planning Consultant
Caret Associates, Inc.

Janet Lareau
Corporate Benefits Coordinator
Kemper National Insurance Co.

Eddie Murphy
Manager Retiree Relations
Hughes Aircraft Company

Merrie Kay Sharar
Retirement/Benefits Manager
Sisters of Providence Health System

E. Joan Whiting
Employee Counselor
Mayo Clinic

An Invitation to Join the International Society for Retirement Planning

ISRP welcomes into membership anyone involved in retirement and life planning, education and counseling, and retiree relations. When you join ISRP, you also become a member of the American Society on Aging. As a member, you will enjoy these benefits:

- Subscriptions to five outstanding publications:

  Retirement Planning, the quarterly publication of the International Society for Retirement Planning.

  Perspectives on Retirement, ISRP's quarterly newsletter.

  Generations, the quarterly journal of the American Society on Aging.

  Aging Today, ASA's bi-monthly newspaper.

  Inside ASA, ASA's membership newsletter.

- Discounts of 30% to 40% on all ISRP and ASA conferences.

- Opportunities to develop and expand professional and personal contacts.

- Access to information and resources.

- Opportunities for leadership at the local and national levels.

- A membership certificate suitable for framing.

Annual Membership Cost

- $115 individual

- $295 organizational

Organizational members receive full member benefits for two designated individuals and discounts for three individuals to attend conferences and training events.

Contact Ms. Nancy Luttropp, Executive Director
International Society for Retirement Planning
833 Market Street, Suite 511
San Francisco, CA 94103-1824
(415) 974-9631

Retirement Planning Resources
from Crisp Publications

Available Titles

Comfort Zones, by Elwood N. Chapman. Also available a Leader's Guide, Loose-leaf format and video.

From Work to Retirement, by Marion E. Haynes

The Best of Retirement Planning, by Marion E. Haynes (ed.)

The Unfinished Business of Living, by Elwood N. Chapman

Enhance Your Destiny, by Elwood N. Chapman

Personal Financial Fitness, by Allen Klosowski

Personal Wellness: Your Most Profitable Investment, by Rick Griggs

Order Information

Crisp Publications, Inc.
1200 Hamilton Ave.
Menlo Park, CA 94025-9600
Telephone (415) 323–6100
Fax (415) 323–5800

About the Editor

Marion E. Haynes

Mr. Haynes retired April 1, 1991 following a 35-year career in human resources management with Shell Oil Company. His last position was Pensioner Relations Manager in Houston.

He has been a member of the International Society for Retirement Planning's Board of Directors since 1988 and served as president from 1991 to 1993. He chaired its Editorial Board from 1990 to 1991.

Mr. Haynes lives with his wife, Janice, in Springdale, Arkansas and devotes his time to writing, public speaking, community service, and travel.